950

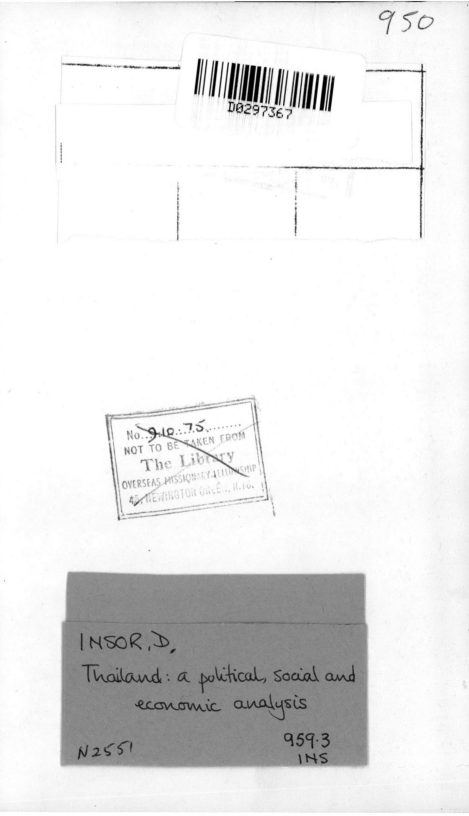

THAILAND

THAILAND

A POLITICAL
SOCIAL, AND ECONOMIC ANALYSIS

❧❀❀❧

BY D. INSOR

Old societies are changing their ways in order to create and maintain a national personality on the world scene, and to bring to their peoples the benefits modern technology can offer. . . . The introduction of modern technology brings about not merely new methods of production but a new style of family life, new links between the villages and the cities, the beginnings of national politics, and a new relationship to the world outside.

w. w. ROSTOW, *in an address*
July 3, 1961

ILLUSTRATED

London
GEORGE ALLEN & UNWIN LTD

RUSKIN HOUSE   MUSEUM STREET

ACKNOWLEDGEMENTS

This study could not have been written without the work of many others, as is recorded within. The author acknowledges permission by The University of Chicago Press to reprint certain extracts from *Siam in Transition* by K. P. Landon. Finally, an invaluable source of information is provided by the reports of the *Bangkok Post*, founded in 1946, supplemented since 1957 by the *Bangkok World*.

﹥⬧❀﹤

FIRST PUBLISHED IN 1963
SECOND IMPRESSION 1965

PRINTED IN GREAT BRITAIN
in 11 point Baskerville type
BY JOHN DICKENS AND CO LTD
NORTHAMPTON

FOREWORD

This book is basically about politics. Politics in Thailand is not
as complex as in the West, but it arises from very different habits,
traditions and ideas. The effects of a cheerful, casual nature, of a
warm climate and a largely rice-growing economy are strongly
marked. Not less noticeable is the pervasive influence of Buddhism. For a Western reader these have first to be described
before considering the political resultant.

There is a further consideration. Study of politics is of necessity
somewhat abstract and de-personalized—though this applies less
to Thailand than to the West. But politics as a human activity
(and as a result of material conditions) can be better understood
when it is approached by way of the city, the village, houses,
food, habits and ideas of the Thai people. This is a circular
approach from living conditions to political behaviour and, at
the same time, from personal observation to political analysis.

The book is in three main parts: (1) general survey; (2)
politics and foreign policy; and (3) economic change.

Thai names: these are usually written in English either as they
are pronounced or as they are transliterated from the Thai. Sarit
Thanarat (as pronounced) is officially Srisdi Dhanarajata (transliteration). Names within appear more or less according to pro-
nunciation. 'Ph' and 'th' indicate aspirated 'p' and 't'—unlike
English usage—as in Phao and Thai. 'Pibun' appears in many
forms—Phibul, Pibulsonggram, Piboon—but here the simplest
has been preferred.

'Thailand' is the official name of the country and corresponds
to the name used in Thai. 'Siam' refers to the Kingdom rather
than the country, and has been superseded except among Europeans. Kings were Absolute Monarchs until 1932 and are now
Constitutional. The present ruler is King Phumipon Adunyadet,
or Rama IX, known also informally as *Nai Luang*, the 'lord
within (the Palace)'.

Personalities:

Marshal Sarit—Prime Minister (since 1959), Supreme Commander of the Armed Forces (since 1957), leader of the Revolutionary Party (October 1958).

Marshal Pibun—former Prime Minister (1938–44, 1948–57), 'Promoter' of the coup ending Absolute Monarchy (1932), in exile in Japan since 1957.

Police-General Phao—former Director-General of Police (1948–57), former Minister of the Interior (1957), in exile in Switzerland since 1957, died November 1960.

Nai Pridi—civilian, former Prime Minister (1946), 'Promoter' of the coup ending Absolute Monarchy, in exile in China since 1949. (First names are generally used in Thailand. *Nai* in this case means Mr.)

The Country:

Buddhist in religion, Hindu in culture (Sanskrit classical literature, Brahminic rites), Chinese in origin (Thai tribes migrated from Southern China a thousand years ago).

Neighbours: Burma, Laos, Cambodia (Khmer) and Malaya.

Population: twenty-seven million, including three million Chinese.

Capital: Bangkok, over two million inhabitants.

Chief Occupation: rice-farming (Thai), trading (Chinese).

National income: equivalent of £34 sterling or $100 US a year a head.

Currency: baht or *tical* (1 baht=4d. or 5 cents; in round figures 20 baht (strictly 21)=$1; 60 baht=£1.

Note: Since this book was published, early in 1963, there have been certain changes, though more in personalities than policies. Marshal Sarit died in December 1963, bequeathing a major financial scandal to the nation. (His former chief, Marshal Pibun, died not long afterwards). General (now Marshal) Thanom succeeded Sarit as Prime Minister, while the ambitious General Prapart became Deputy Prime Minister and Army Commander-in-Chief. Pote Sarasin left SEATO to take over the important Ministry of National Development. Several Air Marshals were arrested a year later for "plotting" against the regime, and tension continues in the North-East. But the economic boom goes on and elections may be held – for the first time in eight years – late in 1965.

CONTENTS

ILLUSTRATIONS

INTRODUCTION

THAI AND FARANG

Only the Moors (Moslems), the Chinese, French and English live in the City, all the other Nations are lodged in the environs by camps. . . .
Trade of foreign merchants was formerly very good . . . but for some years, the various revolutions in China, Japan and India prevented foreign merchants coming in great numbers.

(Chevalier de Chaumont, 1686)

The word *farang*, or Westerner, originated three centuries ago when French influence, engendered by Louis XIV, was dominant in Thailand. French priests had the ear of the king, Narai; French troops were guarding the river fortresses; and Constantine Phaulkon, Greek adventurer and leading figure at the court of Siam, was wholly behind the foreign power. The death of King Narai in 1688 shattered their designs: Phaulkon was executed and the French expelled, and Western influence was not restored for 150 years.

Although the word *farang* derives from *français* (*farangsed* in Thai), it carries few undertones of the imperialist past. Criticism is still implied when you hear of alleged 'pressure by *farang* oil companies', accidents caused by '*farang* drivers' and so on. But when small children chant '*farang*, *farang*' or, as often, '*F'lang, f'lang*', there is no association of 'foreigner' with 'outside interference'.

It is a tribute to Thai tolerance and goodwill that there is so little unpleasantness of that sort. For in fact nearly all *farang* enjoy a highly privileged status in Thailand. Those who in their own countries belong to the middle classes find themselves in the highest social circles: they dine with the wealthy and associate with the aristocracy. They have large cars, modern houses, a staff of servants—drivers, gardeners, cooks, wash amahs, houseboys—because their incomes are so much above the average Thai level (they may earn in a day what they pay one of their servants in a month).

White supremacy dies hard; yet it is the Westerner who looks out of place in Thailand. 'Eyes like rice water', the Thais say of westerners; 'red-haired devils', the Chinese call them. Thais possess a charm almost unknown to the West, though what abilities they have they get mostly from the Chinese. Bangkok itself is largely a Chinese town—the result of settlement and inter-marriage.

In contrast to the barren or over-crowded lands of much of Asia, Thailand is fortunate. The people live by the presence of water, which mitigates the effect of the sun; even the poorest labourers—men and women—take a dip several times a day. Children go to school in freshly starched white shirts or blouses. In a hot climate neatness and cleanliness are virtues, but are also personal disciplines which avert stagnation.

Thais are masters of unconcern: '*Mai pen rai*' ('Never mind') is almost the first phrase a foreigner learns. *Farang*, bringing their worries and problems with them from the West, discover how to relax (if they don't it may be fatal, for Thailand can at times be exasperating). Perhaps because of this attitude, most Thais look astonishingly young, as do most other South-East Asians: it is rare to see a very aged person. *Sanuk* (fun, amusement) comes naturally to them; not being sought directly, even happiness can be found.

Co-operation rather than competition is their way of life. It is not good to hurt people's feelings. They are not direct (the Westernized ones, perhaps, excepted); but they are devious, ambiguous, reserved; it is difficult to know their true feelings and a political conversation is almost impossible; it is always carried on in terms of personalities rather than concepts—but so is Thai politics.

Never colonized, accepting only as much of the West as rulers and people thought fit, the Thais are perhaps the last of the orientals.

CHAPTER I

BANGKOK

⊰⊹⊱

ENTRY

You may enter Bangkok by road, rail, sea or air, and Don Muang Airport is the largest in South-East Asia. It lies on the round-the-world route between Calcutta and Tokyo, and is more convenient than Rangoon, Saigon or Singapore. Above all, Thailand is 'stable' (no civil strife), pro-Western (so far) and picturesque (canals, temples and palaces).

The airport is about fifteen miles north of Bangkok, just off the northern highway which leads ultimately to Chiangmai. Unlike most roads in Bangkok, which change their names every few hundred yards (i.e. at crossroads), the north-south highway bears one name throughout its 450-mile length: Bahon Yothin Road, named after the Prime Minister of the 1930's.

In the short drive from the airport to the capital, one can see much of Thailand in miniature. The countryside is flat, paddy fields stretching to the horizon, broken only by clumps of bamboos and isolated palm leaf huts, raised on stilts along the line of the road. The rice shoots, newly planted after the first rains of June or July, are brilliant green; small dikes separate each flooded field. Peasant girls in canoes or men and women with wicker traps catch fish in the ponds and swamps beside the road. Small boys and girls lie astride grazing buffaloes. 'There is rice in the fields, fish in the water' is the most enduring of Thai sayings.

Approaching Bangkok, the fields give way to multi-coloured town houses, owned by rich Thais and usually rented to foreigners, interspersed with the traditional palm thatch or teak wood dwelling. Shade trees meet in an arch over the road, which is being widened. In Thailand, this is an unusual sight, for few roads are well built or decently maintained: it is usual to wait for holes to appear and then to patch them up with stones and a little tar. Canals follow the road most of the way; they were the original means of transport before roads were developed, but now canals in Bangkok are being filled in with earth so that wider roads can take their place.

Across the fields a big cement plant can be seen; it is managed by a Dane and is one of Thailand's few industries. On the opposite side are army barracks, a fitting reminder of martial law, imposed by Marshal Sarit on launching the 'Revolution' of October 1958. The presence of the Army is not unduly obtrusive, and it arouses little popular apprehension. But it does demonstrate where effective control lies, as it has done for most of the past twenty or twenty-five years.

Back towards the airport is a large temple, the *Wat Mahatat*, or irreverently 'Wat Pibun', modelled after the beautiful Marble Temple in Bangkok built by King Chulalongkorn just over fifty years ago. *Wats* (monasteries) are still founded by pious villagers, wealthy citizens or aspiring politicians. Just as the people rub little gold-leaf squares on to the images of the Buddha for luck, so politicians and others hope to derive material benefits from their acts of merit: the act—whatever the intention—still seems to count in rural eyes.

Further on are signs of secular progress: the large and impressive architecture of the Agricultural University. The Thais have created in their public buildings a genuine synthesis of the art of East and West. Long, sloping roofs, often of green tiles, slightly overlapping at the ends, derive from the characteristic three or four tiered temple roofs. The University also sells chickens and turkeys, vegetables, plants and flowers to the public; prices are fixed, unlike those of the city markets and of most shops, where bargaining is the rule.

Markets, food stalls, shops, huts and mansions—and then the obelisk, the 'Victory Monument' or, as it is splendidly called in Thai: *Anusawari Chaisamorapoom*. Like most dignified, commemorative or abstract words, this is not really Thai but Sanskrit—reflecting two thousand years of Hindu influence in South-East Asia. The victory, incidentally, was over French forces in Indo-China in 1941: it was more or less stage-managed by the Japanese, who later occupied both sides. Marshal Sarit won his spurs in this struggle. Marshal Pibun, his predecessor, won his as long ago as 1932 as a 'promoter' of the coup that ended absolute monarchy. Every year there is a ceremony at the Victory Monument. It is said that one year Marshal Pibun invited a French representative to attend, among others (as SEATO allies), which he did. Both had forgotten the origins of the victory! Though in fact it had been little more than a border scuffle, the repercussions still plague the 'Golden Peninsula' to this day. Towards the end of the last century, the French had seized large tracts under Thai suzerainty in Laos and bombarded Bangkok in the process; they had also restored four provinces—including the celebrated Angkor Wat—to Cambodia. Thailand regained these possessions during the last war and lost them again after the Japanese surrender.

THE COMMERCIAL CENTRE

Bangkok, like most of Thailand, is flat. There is a difference of no more than a few feet in height between any two points. This creates a tremendous drainage problem as there is nowhere for flood water to flow, and the water level is already close to the surface. The annual rainfall is about 55 inches (as compared with 30 inches in England), but it is concentrated into five or six monsoon months, from May to October. Even in the rainy season there is never a continuous drizzle, but sudden, short tropical downpours.

Bangkok's flatness is matched by the flatness of the surrounding countryside—in acres and acres of rice fields stretching far into the north. Even within the city, shops, offices and houses follow the horizontal trend. Looking down towards the main town from the centre-north, near the King's Palace, only Government House, the 'needle' of a nearby *chedi* or a shrine for relics and the 'spire' of the Golden Mount (a temple erected on an artificial hill) break the line of the trees.

Alluvial deposits of silt brought down by the river have given the city unstable foundations, making it expensive to erect buildings of more than four or five storeys. Shortage of capital for development is another factor; wealth still goes into land, valuables, money-lending and gambling rather than into industry or commerce.

In the business centre, the oldest part of Bangkok, most shops open out of long two-storey terraces. New Road, the longest and oldest street in town—formerly an elephant track—is an extraordinary patchwork of yellowish or off-white terrace shops, their Victorian-style classical mouldings barely discernible beneath the grime. Canvas or cotton awnings, with faded advertisements, droop from the projecting concrete ledges separating each shop from the dwelling above. Thick, ugly telephone poles support a profusion of wires. Antiquated trams still trundle past.

New Road is the tourist street. Shops sell silver bowls and ornaments, niello-silver cigarette boxes, zircons (Thai diamonds), star sapphires, 'princess' rings, crocodile skins, teak elephants and Thai silk ties. There are tailors—most of them Chinese, some Vietnamese—restaurants (again mostly Chinese) and nightclubs, now quite respectable.

New Road ('Progress of the City' is its Thai name) meanders through the commercial section, which is almost solidly Chinese. Further out, blocks of terraced shops (hong taew—'row of rooms'—in Thai), alternate with houses, temple compounds and 'jungle' wastes. Even Petburi Road, a modern six-lane highway, is bordered by old-fashioned wooden stores, a disused field filled with sacks of charcoal, water jars that encroach on to the pavement, new concrete shopping blocks in gay colours, European style dwellings, a couple of embassies and clusters of small wooden houses. Behind ceremonial Rajadamnoen Avenue, flanked by office buildings and government ministries, are innumerable wooden shacks and hovels. Many poor families, perhaps one-seventh of all the families in the city, live in a single room or even a part of a room or in a shed.

There are few modern 'built-up' streets in Bangkok; one of them is Patpong Road. Twenty years ago it was a piece of waste land that could be bought for sixty thousand baht, but today it is worth twenty million (one million dollars). It is lined by smart restaurants, air line offices, beauty salons and the US Information Services. Lately, there has been a great increase in activity in Bangkok: wooden shops and houses were taken down and replaced by new shopping blocks in smart colours; a new luxury hotel (the Rama) was built, roads were widened, parking meters installed, playing fountains erected. But the traditional pattern still predominates. With the exception of a few stores owned by Thai, Indians or other foreigners, the prevalent shop is the Chinese 'shop-all'. This is a 'hole in the wall', its simple, oblong interior crammed with goods. Behind the shop is another, smaller room from which stairs lead up to the grilled and shuttered bedrooms. Half a dozen and more such shops can be found side by side in a single terrace block. On some of them, balconies sprout from the bedroom level. Wooden 'fences' fan out between the shops to separate one property from the next. Little children, almost naked, play on the pavement in front of the blocks or in the dark, narrow lanes between them. The women wear silky Chinese trousers, black and baggy; the men wear trousers or shorts.

It is a peculiarity of Bangkok that in certain streets, or sizeable sections of them, only one article is sold. There is a street where only bicycles are sold, where shop after shop is filled with the same gleaming new models; in another street one can buy only modern wash-basins and lavatories in pink, green or white; others offer coffins, hollowed out from tree trunks; or smart watches, clocks and fountain pens; officers' caps and uniforms; basket work of all sorts; brass images of the Buddha, monks' robes and gilded 'altar' tables; water pumps, used in foreign houses, for the supply is unreliable; silver and jewellery; gaily-coloured bales of cottons and silks, sold by Pakistanis or Indians; and false teeth and foot-operated dentists' drills (made in Japan). Other typical Bangkok shops are grocery shops, selling tinned milk, packaged bread, sweets in big glass bottles, biscuits, eggs and detergents ('Omo', 'Fab' and 'Tide' are household names in Bangkok); shoe shops, dressmakers, dry-cleaners (displaying shark-skin suits in the window); shops with little girls' short flounced dresses, pink, red, blue, white or green, spread outside like butterflies; padded bras for Asian figures; gloomy Chinese drug stores, with rhinoceros horns (for grinding), dried snakes and frogs and curious roots and powders; chemist shops where even dangerous drugs are supplied without prescription and no doubt imitation medicines

B

too (every so often a 'factory' is spotted by the police and closed down).

Manufactories of water jars or 'spirit houses' can be found everywhere in Bangkok. There are shops making buckets or watering cans. There are radio and television shops, for Bangkok has two television networks—Thai and Army TV— and there is talk of a third, to be sponsored by the police, that will televise in colour! There are mirror-makers and picture-framers, photography shops showing glamorous girls or uniformed officials, bookshops and magazine stalls (more pretty girls), and hairdressers and barber shops. Hardware shops are packed with Chinese bowls and plates, some still in their paper wrappings and strung from the walls, with others piled up on packing cases; lanterns, buckets and lengths of rope hang from the ceiling. Chinese eating houses have glass showcases in front, exposing glossy yellow chickens, hanging meat, offal of all kinds (nothing is wasted in Chinese cooking), green spring onions and white noodles. The cook stands at his white-tiled charcoal oven, slicing meat and vegetables; customers dip chop-sticks into bowls of rice.

Only foreign firms, government offices, banks, cinemas, temples, hotels and hospitals provide breaks in the almost end-less lines of horizontal, terraced structures. Gigantic and highly-coloured figures advertise the cinemas, of which there are half a dozen that are new, comfortable and air-conditioned, showing Thai or Western films at a top price of just over five shillings (75 cents). Most of them show epic, cowboy or crime films. In the smaller cinemas naughty Japanese films are popular, and Indian romances, if spoken in Thai. There is no real dubbing; the sound track is cut, and in the cinema actors speak the lines.

Banks are as dignified as they are everywhere, but people do not save and prefer to take their money to shops that sell gold belts, chains and bracelets. Some look like glass palaces, rising high into the air; only the ground floor is open up to the curved red-lined counter behind which the assistants display their wares. Belts and chains of various sizes and forms hang from the walls on curtains of gold. Savings are usually invested in gold—but Thai women hide their belts beneath skirts and blouses for fear of thieves. Only in Laos, where civilization has hardly spread, do the women and girls openly wear their dazzling gold or silver belts.

Hotels vary from simple wooden houses dimly lettered in Chinese and Thai to vast concrete air-conditioned edifices that charge over four pounds ($12) a day for a single room without meals. Few hotels—except for the half-dozen or so that cater to foreign tourists—are more respectable than anywhere else in the East. A Thai-English phrase book even points a finger at what was then 'the best hotel in town' and adds: 'I want to enjoy myself with a woman. Can you get one for me?' Girls can also be taken to hired houses outside Bangkok invitingly labelled 'Hotel Friendship' or 'Bungalow Home Fun'.

TEMPLES

With saffron robes and shaven heads, Buddhist monks hold out their rice bowls every morning to be filled. They eat before noon, taking no food for the rest of the day. On holy days (the *Wan Phra*), which accord with the four phases of the moon, sermons are delivered in the temples. On special festivals, men and women gather with lotus buds, scented water and incense sticks to offer to the image of the Buddha; in the evening, following the scripture readings and the sermon, a candle-light procession circles the temple building three times.

This main building, called the *Bot*, has the characteristic three or four layers of roofs, overlapping in the Chinese style. Their gilded eaves writhe in the shape of the *naga*—the king cobra—a symbol of great significance in Asia. Ceremonial lions guard the entrance. Within, the walls are painted with scenes from the life of the Buddha or, quite often, scenes from the Hindu *Ramayana*—the popular legend of Rama, his wife Sita and the giant who abducts her to the isle of Lanka (Ceylon) and is there defeated by the forces of Rama and the monkey-general Hanuman. At the far end is the main image of the Buddha, sometimes of great size, often in the posture of overcoming temptation: the left arm folded, the right extended and the hand touching the ground to attest to the good deeds of this and previous lives.

Thai images of the Buddha are famous, particularly those in

the classical style of Sukhotai, first Thai capital (thirteenth and fourteenth centuries). The delicate oval face, topped by the flame-like *usnisa* (sign of enlightenment), the half-closed eyes and gentle smile present an ideal of serenity, contemplation and compassion. After Sukhotai, the capital was established at Ayuthaya for more than four hundred years, until the city was destroyed by the Burmese. The late Ayuthaya style—with its large, rather empty features—is considered one of decadence, but it suits the copying industry which has grown up to meet the current demand for antiques.

In Bangkok there are said to be three hundred Buddhist temples. The most famous, extravagant and spectacular of them all is the *Wat Phra Keo*, Temple of the Emerald Buddha, in the compound of the Grand Palace, surrounded by great high battlemented walls like a Tibetan monastery.

The Emerald Buddha, brought to Bangkok after a series of miraculous adventures, is now the most celebrated image of its kind. To swear by it is to take the most sacred oath. A certain politician, recently removed from power, was said to have been challenged before the Emerald Buddha to deny his part in some misdoing; this he did, and so was punished, people say, for his perfidy. The image itself is small and barely visible in the recesses of the temple, mounted high on a gilded structure, surrounded by golden images of standing Buddhas, while slender umbrellas, one above the other and diminishing in size with each tier, represent the kings and lesser royalty. Little gold and silver trees stand in glass cases, tribute to the Thai kings from Lao princes. Gifts from other royal houses and travel souvenirs are placed haphazardly here and there.

The outward splendour and magnificence of the temple buildings and their adornments belong to a world of fantasy. On one side golden *garudas*, the legendary mount of Vishnu, half-man, half-bird; on the other giants, twenty feet high, brightly painted, with savage, grinning faces and protruding tusks. A golden *chedi* rises high in the air. Small shrines appear, encrusted in gold. Temple bells sound in the breeze.

Nearby stands *Wat Poh*, temple of the reclining Buddha, an enormous image of brick and concrete, finished with gold, 150 feet long and nearly 40 feet high. *Wat Poh* is also known for its marble plaques decorated in high relief with scenes from the Ramayana. Small boys can be seen at work with rice paper and oils producing 'rubbings' which they sell at 20 baht a sheet. Chinese statues of mandarins, lions and other beasts stand stiffly at various aspects of the temple. Two tall statues, also in stone, of a bearded, goggling, vaguely medieval figure are imagined to be of Marco Polo, when resident at the court of Kublai Khan. In odd contrast is a *lingam* stone, with smouldering sticks of incense, emblem of fertility in the cult of Shiva, brought over from Cambodia and still worshipped to this day.

The third of the great temples of Bangkok is *Wat Benchama-bopit*, temple of the fifth King, the famous Chulalongkorn, who reigned for over forty years. This majestic temple, built in the early years of this century, is entirely of white marble but for the glazed tiles of the overlapping roofs and their glittering eaves. Small grey dragons are barely visible in the recesses of the eaves; they were put there by Chinese masons who could not resist adding their own distinctive contribution. Richly decorated windows in red and gold stand out against the pure marble of the walls.

Such are the great temples of Bangkok, not to mention *Wat Arun*, temple of the dawn; or *Wat Sutat*, a place of refuge during the last war's bombing of Bangkok; or *Wat Trai Mitr*, with its newly discovered Buddha of gold, cased in cement to save it from the Burmese. They inspired Bishop Pallegoix to write a hundred years ago this observation, which is equally true today.

'Rising into the air,' he writes in the *Description du Royaume Thai ou Siam*, 'are golden shrines, domes, high pyramids, admirably built, with designs of porcelain in all colours; the overlapping roofs of pagodas, decorated with fine carvings and covered with varnished tiles, reflect the rays of the sun. Several thousands of floating shops, mounted on rafts, following the winding course of the majestic river . . . ; the fortress white as snow, the town with its towers and numerous gates; the lines of canals which traverse the city, the golden spire of the palace with its four-fold facade, the variety of buildings in Indian, Chinese or European style; the individual costumes of the various nations, the sound of music, the songs from plays, the movement and life of this great city. . . .'

TRANSPORT

As a guide book says, 'Bangkok is a spread out town and nobody can tell you where the centre is.' Outside the main commercial area, a house and compound may stand next to a row of shops, wooden huts or waste land. Roads like this extend for miles, separating the area of government offices and the Grand Palace from the embassy area and from the main residential district. 'Less than sixty years ago,' W. A. Graham wrote in 1924, 'there were no streets, the sole means of communication being by boat or on elephant-back along tracks which were soft mud when the tide was out and runnels of water when it was in.'

Now the rich go by car. Private cars increased in number from 4,500 in 1947 to 35,000 ten years later. Huge American cars, some of them air-conditioned, the fashionable Mercedes-Benz, British, French, Italian and Japanese models can all be seen.

Add to this some 8,000 taxis (London has 6,000) all until recently without meters: even with meters it is customary to bargain for one's fare before entering. Taxi driving is a 'reserved' occupation—reserved, that is, for Thai nationals and not 'alien' Chinese. Each driver must wear a peaked cap, though shoes, evidently, are optional. Most taxis are owned by big companies which hire them out for the day. A taxi driver may earn as much as 130 baht (over £2 or $6) a day—less 60 baht or more for hire; but the average net wage, so the police stated early in 1961, comes to only 20 or 30 baht (7s. to 10s. or $1 to $1.50) a day. Rent for a room in a small wooden house in a crowded, narrow lane, without water or electricity, may be as little as 60 baht a month.

Taxi driving has its occupational risks—not just accidents, which are common enough. Hooligans, late at night in a deserted place, may rob, wound and even kill the driver. One September night, for example, a taxi driver drove a couple from Lumpini Park, named after the Buddha's birthplace, to a bridge in the north. As soon as they got out, four men waiting there asked him to return. Near the Bangkok water works, 'they asked him to stop (according to the police report) and get out of the taxi. They beat and kicked him, tied him up, took 235 baht (nearly £4 or $12) from him, and drove his taxi away'. A quarter of an hour later, another taxi driver picked up three men who asked him to stop in Convent Road. 'They tied him up, gagged him with a lemon and put him in the rear of the car. . . . When Lye Huat (the driver) saw a police patrol passing by, he kicked open the door and fell out. The three men drove on.'

It was a passing *samlor* driver who freed the first victim. *Samlors* (tricycle-rickshaws) were invented in 1933; variants are still in use all over Asia. In Thailand the driver pedals in front, the passengers sit in a little cab behind. A hood can be drawn up to give shade and canvas panels are let down when it rains. The *samlor* driver himself, usually in worn black shorts and shirt, and wearing a straw hat (compulsory), often has no other protection. Fortunately for him, the country is flat.

Most *samlor* drivers come from the poverty-stricken northeast. They can make about 30 baht a day; this is more than unskilled hard labouring and their time is their own. It used to be common in Bangkok to see them at midday, fast asleep in their *samlors*.

In 1960 *samlors* were banned in Bangkok, though they are still used up-country. There were as many as 13,000 registered vehicles and some 15,000 drivers, but they obstructed the traffic too much, the government said. So, after nine months' warning, a complete ban was imposed. Drivers were offered land for farming, resettlement in the north-east, or public works construction.

Japanese motorized three-wheelers replaced them. They carry goods in Japan, people in Thailand—varying from two to six or eight passengers. Costing about 20,000 baht each, and brightly coloured for the local market, they are driven with verve. So many were being imported for use in Bangkok that the government had to refuse to permit any more. Their number is now fixed at 7,000.

Buses, desperately overcrowded, often old and of wood, dangerously creaking and swaying, rush on their long and roundabout journeys competing for fares. The Ministry of Communications in 1958 planned to improve Bangkok's bus services through more efficient control of the bus lines and by the end of 1961 the government had approved the municipality taking over all bus concessions gradually. The chief trouble was the existence of too many small companies; 'they usually keep buses at starting points until they are packed with both sitting and standing passengers, and when at last they leave on their routes there is no space left for prospective passengers waiting at bus stops'.

The total number of buses in 1960 was just over 2,000 for a population of over two million; but the number of bus companies had been reduced from thirty-two to twenty-eight since 1958. There are forty-eight different routes. It is curious that the various companies—White Bus Company, Express Transport Organization, red, yellow and green companies, to name a few—number their buses as they enter service and only recently, in small figures, according to routes.

Driving habits are lax. Few signals are given, except for turns and the customary 'hand-off' to keep back approaching traffic; vehicles pull out or cut in quite casually and often without looking. Taxis are the worst offenders, as there is an almost universal desire to impress the passengers with a furious turn of speed. Driving may be hazardous, as frequent scattered glass and occasional overturned taxis bear witness, but there are no displays of anger or resentment as in Europe.

Unfortunately, many taxis and a good proportion of private cars are not insured; when people are injured they may have no financial redress. Court cases can drag on for months and false witnesses are not unknown.

Breakdowns seem to be fewer than before, but a bus often gets stuck with all its passengers aboard while the driver and an assistant squat on the mudguards peering hopefully into the engine. Or a taxi is left jacked up at one side while the driver goes off (no spares) to get the wheel repaired. Favourite spots for breakdowns—for Thais are careless about maintenance—are level crossings: the main railway station is in the middle of town and passenger trains pass through all day. As the striped posts jerkily descend, with a warning clang at every jerk, cars draw to a halt and sometimes cannot be restarted.

The roads themselves do not contribute to smooth running. They are constantly patched but rarely repaired, but roads are being widened in many places. Gangs of workers, paid at

15 baht (5s. or 75 cents) a day, fill in the canals, cut wayside trees, break up stones and lay pipes.

This is progress in Bangkok. The shade trees have been cut down; first the branches, all the way along the street, then the thick trunks. Standing at one of the empty spaces, the telephone posts, burdened with wires, have a remote surrealist air. Like main street in a mid-western town, you see only wooden shacks, dust and mud sidewalks.

Further down the road are piles of timber, trenches and embankments, concrete drainage tubes, concreting machines and men and women digging in the mud. At one point women in long skirts and long-sleeved blouses, with coloured cloths around their heads, mud-spattered and dusty, form a human chain to toss lumps of clay from one to the other.

Yet where the road now runs were canals on either side, with humped wooden bridges, and a small market stood at the corner abutting on to the road itself, selling fried bananas, other fruit and snacks, under the shade of the trees.

UP COUNTRY

The population of Bangkok, with Thonburi, is under two and a half million. Ten times this number live up-country, in the rice-growing central plain, in the arid north-east, in the mountainous north, and in the long, straggling part-Malay-speaking peninsula of the south.

Almost half the Thai population, ten million of them, live in boats, floating houses or houses on stilts along the banks of rivers and canals. The main rivers of Thailand, with their tributaries, form a network of waterways over a thousand miles in length, navigable throughout the year. Artificial canals, particularly in Bangkok and the central plain, are nearly as long. Eighty-seven per cent of the total rice production is moved from the paddy fields to the mills and storage depots by these waterways.

Canals in Bangkok form a secondary communications system. Some are as wide as rivers and all kinds of launches, passenger boats and 'sampans'—rowed forward and stuffed with charcoal, household supplies or fruit and vegetables—ply up and down. Often there are canals on one or even both sides of the streets, giving them a very picturesque appearance, for there are usually trees, bushes and shrubs wherever there is water, while narrow wooden bridges lead to the houses on the other side.

Approaching Bangkok by air you see teak, bamboo or leaf huts, usually with corrugated iron roofs, strung out along the roadways or the streams and canals, surrounded by coconut palms, banana plants and mango trees. Beyond these narrow fringes of settlement stretch the innumerable rectangular rice fields, with an occasional farm house set in a clump of bamboos. Rivers are the life blood of Thailand, providing irrigation for the fields, fish for the farmers and baths for men, women, children and buffaloes alike.

No up-country town can rival Bangkok in size or importance. Even Chiangmai, the historic capital of the north, has a population of only 100,000. Korat in the north-east, linked with the northern highway by a new American road ('Friendship Highway'), is a small provincial town with a few bazaar streets, some government buildings and an open square by the old fortress gateway where movies can be shown at night. Songkla, the main port in the south, is still cut off by road from Bangkok, though jeeps can get through in the dry season.*

Less than forty years ago, there were 'very few roads anywhere in Siam', Graham reports, 'and none at all in the central part. Travelling up-country, by boat, on foot or elephant back, took days.' Henri Mouhot, the French explorer who discovered Angkor Wat, describes his journey from Bangkok to Luang Prabang a hundred years ago:

'Most villages,' he writes, 'are a day's march one from another; but sometimes one goes three or four days before meeting a single habitation; then one is forced to stay in the jungle. In the good season this might be pleasant; but during the rains, nothing can give an idea of the sufferings that travellers undergo at night, sheltered only by a poor barrier of leaves hastily put

* Railways link Bangkok with Songkla and Malaya; to the north, with Chiangmai; in the north-east, with Korat and (by ferry) Vientiane; and with Cambodia. The 'death-railway' to Burma is no longer maintained. Air services also link the main towns.

up above a bed of branches, assailed by myriads of mosquitoes attracted by the light of torches and fires, legions of horseflies which . . . attack man as well as beast, almost invisible midges which surround you in swarms, and whose bite is exceedingly painful and causes enormous blisters; not to speak of enormous leeches, which at the earliest light, leave the earth, smell man at almost twenty paces and from all sides come at an incredible speed to suck his blood. . . .'

The journey to the north has none of these hazards. The main road joins the towns, and the villages spring up beside the road. The road brings civilization, or at least its universal substitute, money. Before the Friendship Highway was built, the Korat plateau exported about 10,000 tons of maize; two years later it sold well over 200,000 tons a year, worth £5 million ($15 million)—nearly the cost of the road itself. No-one could call the northern highway such a good road, but for the traveller it provides a passage from Chiangmai to Bangkok through the heart of the country.

Chiangmai is a neat, well-swept, orderly town with clean peasant huts on the outskirts; there are traditional silver-making and lacquerware villages and an excellent covered market selling meat and fish (all screened), fruit and vegetables, sweets and cakes, baskets, flowers and little green parrots for seven shillings (one dollar) each. Two bridges span the broad but shallow river, Me Ping, and in the evening children come down to paddle and swim. By the crumbling brick walls of the old town there are many temples, some with beautiful ornate carvings in the Burmese style. Elephants are usually at work in the nearby teak forests from dawn to 11 a.m., but in the hot-season (March to May) they rest. Karens, Miaos, Kamuks and other tribespeople live in the hills to the north and west, where they burn the forests and grow opium. There is a heat haze at this season, and the mountains are lost in the mist.

Outside Chiangmai are plots of green vegetables and the dry squares of the rice fields. Cows are tethered to posts by long sticks, painted bullock carts lumber along the road, and to irrigate their fields peasants scoop out water with shovels. Small boys lead the family buffalo to graze, buses rush past with their roofs laden with goods and bicycles, while men and women walk to their houses carrying water in kerosene tins.

About forty miles south of Chiangmai you enter scrub forest with burnt clearings; huts are never very far away, raised on stilts, with pigs and fowls scratching underneath, with grey thatched roofs, and wooden or leaf-woven walls. The school and its flag post are conspicuous in every village. There is one primary school—usually housed in a monastery or temporary building—with 150 pupils and four or five teachers, to every thousand people in Thailand. The road is a dirt-track with narrow log bridges over the dry gullies. By the roadside girls and men wait patiently for buses.

Twenty miles on, a grey, stony road passes through the bare forest, the earth scored with dried-up river tracks. A wide, American concrete bridge has been built; others are in construction. The Americans are rebuilding or replacing about a thousand bridges throughout Thailand; without them the roads would be torn away during the rains. Sometimes a bus breaks down and four or five men look hopefully at the engine; the passengers sit and wait. Teak saplings, rice fields, tobacco plants, sewing machines in the bigger village huts. Groups of people watch one from the local store.

There are road sweepers every few miles; they wear topees, khaki shorts or trousers; they throw sand on to bad patches and rake out loose stones. Their bicycles, with food and water in bamboo sticks, lie near them. Bicycles as well as buses are to the Asian peasant perhaps the most significant of Western inventions. Forty years ago, or less, many of these people would never have moved beyond their villages in their lives.

Eighty miles from Chiangmai and the dense forest draws near; nearly half the land is under forest. Teak logs are stacked by the roadside. A beautiful, white-washed temple, with red eaves, is just visible between the trees. It was probably built in 1957, for the 2,500th anniversary of the birth of Buddha. Every large village, or group of villages, has its own wat, or temple, often with columns and steeply sloping roof. The village abbot is the customary source of advice, lay and spiritual—though the headman or district officer now officially dispenses justice.

Rice fields appear again. Water buffaloes, with young, stolidly graze. (Buffaloes are valuable, costing £20 (nearly $60) or more. In pre-war China a buffalo cost twice as much to hire as a man.) Boys, wearing only the ubiquitous *pakaoma*, a checked cloth wound round the body as a sarong or tucked up to form trunks, or as a turban round the head, or knotted round the waist for emergencies, swim in the stream.

Girls have short permanently waved hair, which thickly clusters round their heads. Only old women now wear the traditional close crop. Around Chiangmai, however, as throughout northern Thailand, Laos and Burma, hair is worn long, brushed back from the face and fixed in a bun. And as in the old days, country women and girls often leave the breasts bare, though brassieres and skirts are more usual in town.

Now the road winds into the mountains among the bare hills, where the forests have been razed. The only traffic is an occasional car, a bus-load of travellers, or a lorry with empty soft drink bottles, for soft drinks are big business in Thailand; Coca Cola and Pepsi Cola, Bireley, Fanta, Seven-Up and Green Spot are on almost every village stall. Only once in the year is the traffic unusual: this is for the *Songkran* Festival in mid-April, the Thai New Year. In Bangkok it is little observed today (the official New Year is January 1st), but in Chiangmai, as in Rangoon, there are three days of Buddhist ceremonies, public processions, dances and water throwing.

Descending into the plain, cars and lorries throw up clouds of white dust from the unmade road. Beyond the small town of Thoen, there are the usual fields of rice, scraggy trees and scrub, then sparse woodlands. In the hot season the leafless trees stand, thin and grey, above the yellow-brown earth; the landscape is drained of colour. For months there has been no rain: all day the sun beats down.

Deforestation is at last causing concern. Marshal Sarit, visiting the north-east, was distressed by the bare patches in the hill country where the forests have been burned by shifting cultivators. Special forest police were set up in 1960 to deal with forest destruction; highway patrols were formed to prevent reckless driving and highway robbery, and to keep overloaded lorries off the road. Most of the overloaded trucks that caused damage to roads in the north were those of timber thieves transporting stolen logs!

Thirty miles from Tak is the turning to the Yanhee Dam, a

large hydro-electric project being built by an American company. Since the building of the dam, Tak has acquired a number of shops, variously stocked with car spares, all sorts of ironmongery, clothes and foodstuffs; there is also an airport and there are two modern concrete hotels. The usual up-country hotel is made of wood and its bedroom walls have open spaces at the top to facilitate the flow of air. It may be cool, but it is rarely quiet. A double room with shower and lavatory costs about forty baht (15s. or $2) a day; without, about twenty.

There are missionaries in Tak. Much of their time is spent treating lepers, for there is little government help. Officially there are 100,000 lepers in Thailand, but the true figure is probably double this; the worst area is the north-east, where the number of lepers is increasing.

Life for the Thais, the missionaries say, is not always as rosy as it seems. With their houses closely packed, everything is audible. The wife next door is unhappy at her husband's infidelities: there are bitter quarrels when he comes home. Another man comes home drunk and beats his wife. Thai men, for the most part, are spoilt. Allowed to do what they like in boyhood, they tend to behave in the same way when married. It is the women, as in many countries, who are patient, enduring and businesslike.

While the missionaries of Tak are chiefly medical workers there are proselytizers about fifty miles to the east, in Sukhotai. They live in the new town, not far from the site of the first Thai capital of the thirteenth and fourteenth centuries—the classic period of Thai art. These missionaries, though nicely housed by local standards, have the melancholy task of broadcasting the Gospel by loudspeaker jeep to all who will hear. After many years in the hot, swampy, airless plain their converts are 'very few'.

Most missionaries, it is true, work among the northern tribespeople, who are animists and who need help, because the government can do little. But it is an almost impossible task, and perhaps a mistaken one, to try to convert the Thai people from their own Buddhist faith. Even if they could grasp the supernatural features of Christianity, which are alien to the strict—though not the popular—interpretation of Buddhism, they would still be confronted with the sharp differences of belief between Catholics and Protestants and often between the Protestants themselves.

After viewing the 'idols' at Sukhotai, travellers may return to spend the night at Tak. Along the line of the river, to the south, woodlands stretch for miles either side of the road; there are few villages. The road is grey and bumpy. Grey dust turns to red and a large modern bridge appears, twenty miles from Tak. To the right is the road to Maesod on the Burmese frontier, a road so narrow and precipitous that traffic has to come and go on alternate days. Then green teak forest and smooth red sandstone road almost to Kampaengphet: clearings for charcoal burning and smoking kilns, then more woods, dry grass and scrub and the hills receding in the distance. Here is the beginning of the great central plain which extends nearly 300 miles south to Bangkok.

Here the road, once metalled, is now a ruin. It is like the rough surface of a rock, a hard ribbed spine of jagged stones, littered with smaller stones prised from foundations, the whole covered with varying layers of dust and sand. Pot holes of different size and depth break out at irregular intervals; there are so many that it is impossible to avoid them.

This sort of 'road' persists, on and off, for nearly fifty miles. There are occasional patches of new surfacing, especially near towns, but no systematic repairs. Bad roads extend to within a hundred miles of Bangkok itself. This is the cost of inadequate maintenance and the starvation of the highway department. Yet the expense of repairs to vehicles, the resulting absence of much motor traffic and the consequent impoverishment of trade and cultivation, costs the country many times what it 'saves' through neglecting its roads.*

The approaches to the important rice and timber trading centre of Nakorn Sawan ('heavenly city'), where two rivers

* There have been, it is true, strong political pressures on the highway department to construct more roads than technical capacity permits. 'Perhaps the most serious outcome,' comments the International Bank mission to Thailand, 'is the waste of resources that results from the heavy toll which the rains take each year on the roads which were built initially to unsatisfactory specifications and subsequently neglected.' On the other hand, highways have more than doubled in the ten years since 1947—they were negligible before 1936—and now total about five thousand miles. Such is the importance of transport and communications that they receive nearly half the total public investment, including foreign aid. The northern highway has now been improved.

join to form the Menam Chaophraya which flows down to the sea, are signalled by the sight of rice mills, and the rice straw piled up on platforms with buffaloes sheltering beneath. Nakorn Sawan is a pleasant town with three modern hotels. Eating curry at a little restaurant, you will be asked where you have come from. From Chiangmai, you say. '*Sanuk mai?* (fun, isn't it?)' they ask. No visit is worth making unless it is fun.

Forty miles down river is Chainat, the site of a big dam and flood control project. There is also an expensive hotel built for tourists: but as no tourists came, because of the distance and the poor roads, so the hotel stands empty, used only by visiting officials—one of the White Elephants of the Pibun regime.

From Chainat the road curves eastwards, past a small airfield, with hills around and newly-made huts of bright yellow straw, and dozens of small wooden bridges, to the old town of Lopburi, once a state capital under the Empire of the Khmers. There remains a famous three-towered temple, perhaps a thousand years old, in which miserable squatters now dwell. Nearby is a shrine to Vishnu, still worshipped, where ugly grey monkeys, many in an advanced state of pregnancy, sit and chatter and steal. Towards the river is the palace of King Narai and the house of Constantine Phaulkon.

Lopburi also shows the effects of Marshal Pibun's improving zeal with its broad two-way highway, imposing roundabouts and tall modern buildings. But Ayuthaya, capital of Siam for four hundred years, shows it to the point of absurdity. A fine tree-lined street, with high concrete buildings on either side, appears out of the wilderness and ends as abruptly as it begins. Beyond are the ruins of ancient palaces and temples, while still further away is the present market town. The romantic image of a huge Buddha in the decadent Ayuthaya style once stood out magnificently from the shattered walls of an old temple. Now, by the Marshal's order, a temple has been built to cover up the image; three *chedis*, hundreds of years old, have been fitted with new cement coats; smooth concrete tops round off battered temple spires.

But all is transitory in this world; nothing matters very much and few things, it is said, matter at all. Allocations for 'reconstructing' Ayuthaya ended the moment Pibun fled. Now they go to modernize Bangkok instead.

A NOTE ON BANGKOK

Bangkok is not what the Thais call their capital; nor do they say 'Menam' for the great river on which it is situated. *Menam*, or more correctly *maenam*, literally 'Mother of waters', just means 'river'. The full name is *Maenam Chaophraya*—an honorary title signifying Lord of Rivers.

Similarly, Bangkok to the Thais is 'Krungthep', city of angels. It is written 'Krungthep, etc.' in Thai script, to denote a dozen or more symbolic titles which follow. Krungthep derives from Sanskrit, the language of the royal court. 'Thep' or 'Thevoda' (Devata in Hindi) are the angels serving the gods in ancient Brahmin cosmology. These gods and angels have been retained as adjuncts to the Buddhist religion, but are not essential to Buddhism. The Buddha himself accepted the tradition without endorsing it: it is akin to those areas of 'silence' which he maintained on certain issues that were not necessary to salvation.

The Buddhist way to *nirvana* ('work out your own salvation with diligence') is open to all men. The Brahminic mysteries were known only to the elect. So throughout South-East Asia Brahminic rites consecrated the King and the nobility while Buddhism became the religion of the people, overlaying the old, but still persisting, beliefs in spirit worship. Krungthep thus receives the highest sanction of Brahminism as the royal capital; within the city, hundreds of Buddhist temples—particularly the Temple of the Emerald Buddha—preserve the Buddhist heritage; while in the compound of every house or building stands the so-called 'spirit house'—*Phra Phum Chao Thi*, or 'owner of the land'—representing the god whom one must propitiate when building on 'his' land. These are the spiritual foundations of the town.

Historically, Bangkok was merely a fortified post on the bend of the river protecting the former capital, Ayuthaya. Bangkok means the place where wild olives grow. In the present city there are many similar district names: Bangkrak, place of love, in the old town; Bangsue, place of honesty, to the north; Bangkapi, place of shrimp paste (manufacture), now the smart residential area; and so on.

So long as Ayuthaya was the capital—named after Ayodhya,

C

the fabulous city in northern India from which the god Rama launched his expedition to conquer Ceylon—Bangkok remained Bangkok, and was known as such to European traders. But Ayuthaya fell to the Burmese after a long siege in the mid-eighteenth century: it was utterly destroyed and the captive population, as was the custom, taken to Burma. A remnant of the Thai army, under the command of a half-Chinese general, Tak Sin, had escaped just before the fall. Tak Sin took refuge in the east, near Cambodia, rallied an army, defeated the Burmese and drove them out of the country, never to return.

Tak Sin became king and made his capital at Thonburi, across the river from Bangkok. After the first valiant years, checking the Burmese on the one side and the Cambodians on the other, King Tak Sin developed megalomania, imagining himself to be a god. One of his commanders, General Chakri, then deposed him and reigned in his stead. He moved the capital to Bangkok, renaming it Krungthep. Tak Sin he put to death in the royal way: he was tied up in a sack and beaten with sandalwood clubs so that royal blood would not be spilled. Chakri, the first of the present dynasty, was later given the title of Rama, as were all his successors.

CHAPTER 2

CONDITIONS

⟶◦⊰❀⊱◦⟵

'The happiness of the people,' Marshal Sarit has observed, echoing Buddhist precepts, 'depends on four materials: a house to live in, clothes to wear, medicines when sick, food.' But all these in turn depend on climate and geography: in this case a tropical climate (with water for irrigation), close to China (but separated by high mountains and jungles) and open to the eastern plains and to the sea. It was from southern China that the Thais themselves came, evading the pressure of Kublai Khan, but it was from India and Ceylon that Buddhism spread peacefully to Thailand, and it was from Cambodia and the Khmer Empire that Hindu culture and Brahmin rites were absorbed.

CLIMATE

A tropical environment may explain much of the present attitudes and past history of the Thais, as of the other peoples of the 'Golden Peninsula'; it may explain the early flowering and maturity of the great culture of Angkor and Sukhotai—based on irrigation, rice cultivation and a large supply of skilled and unskilled labour. The Khmer Empire was itself overthrown by the more vigorous and numerous migrant Thais, while Cambodia was saved from subjection to Thais and Vietnamese only by the eventual protection of the French; and now the Thais, Malays and Vietnamese are themselves subject, at least economically, to the overseas Chinese.

Heat and humidity are the main features of the climate of South-East Asia; the weather is rarely oppressive, but relaxing, enervating. In Bangkok the yearly average is 84°. In the cool season, from about November to February, temperatures rarely drop below 60° (52° in January 1960 was really cold) and seldom above 90°. In the hot season, March to May, temperatures vary from about 80° at dawn to 100° after noon. When the rains come, from May to mid-October, the temperature drops sharply for a time, but then climbs again.

Bangkok and the Centre have 50 inches of rain a year, most of it in the six rainy months. In the South the amount of rainfall is about the same, but in the North and North-East it is only half that amount. Humidity is high throughout the year over much of Thailand. It is warmer in Bangkok than in most other capitals of South-East Asia, but the rainfall is half that of Singapore or Rangoon.

Even in the cool season the climate varies with alternating belts of hot and cold weather—on a good day like the Riviera in early summer, on a bad day like the greenhouses at Kew. In the afternoon, dogs lie outstretched under the trees motionless; people waiting for buses line up in the shade of telegraph poles. Women hold up parcels to protect their faces from the sun.

In the hot season the sun beats down all day; ponds and streams dry up. The early freshness of dawn soon disappears, but a strong breeze blows in the afternoons (and kite competitions are held). Government officials take their annual two weeks by the sea.

The sky darkens in the rainy season; there is a short lull, followed by fierce gusts of wind which presage the oncoming rain. Ponds overflow, the grass is flooded and paths become waterlooged. Canals are swollen to the level of the arched wooden bridges; the roadways become rutted and muddy. Pedestrians pick their way past the pools, and buses splash and flounder. But in an hour or two the storm has passed and the sun comes out again.

FOOD

The word for 'rice' and 'food' in Thai is almost synonymous; *hew khao*, to be hungry, means literally to be hungry for rice. Rice is the staple food of Thailand, and Thai peasants, when breaking up new land, traditionally plant rice even where (as over much of the North-East) they should not.

Rice, dried fish, young shoots, chillie sauce, watercress and bananas are the normal food of the country. Other fruits, of which there is a great variety in Thailand, are either too dear or not available, except in towns. *Nam-pla*, fish sauce, adds strength and flavour to a meagre diet. The Chinese, on the other hand, are avid eaters, especially of pork and many types of fish which the Thais will not touch.

Thais delight in all kinds of snacks—meat preparations, lotus seeds, sugared tamarind, nuts, cakes, fried bananas, crisp noodles, egg yolk 'sprays' and a dozen others. Vendors pass by in boats, or walk past with baskets hanging from shoulder poles, carrying portable ovens, or pedalling by on heavily-loaded tricycles. Every day, along the lanes of the city, comes the waking call of the breakfast pastry-seller, riding his bicycle. Others click bones or ring bells. At midday the soup-kitchen on wheels stops at every house. In the evening comes a trolley, all lit-up, bearing dried squid, mounted in rows: '*Pla myk malaew krab*'.

The Chinese do most of the lane-by-lane selling often for a very small return, for a bowl of soup with chopped meat, vegetable and noodles costs no more than one baht. But Thai women take their share of the market trade too. Coffee shops also play a large part in Thai life, for that is where the man in the street discusses the lottery results, women and even politics. 'Coffee parliaments' they are called.

One of the largest markets in Bangkok was Pratunam ('watergate') until it was torn down to make way for a road. Partly housed in a vast corrugated iron hangar, partly spreading out on both sides of a narrow lane, it opened at one end on to a large canal, the klong Bangkapi, and at the other on to an important junction. It is worth describing in some detail if only for sentimental reasons (it was the best and cheapest market in town).

Within the great shed, gloomy from lack of light, between the twisted posts supporting the roof, lay three or four rows of cement supports. Between them the rough-cast floors ran with water. Above stretched strings of cob-webbed wires on which hung bundles of noodles, red glistening sausages and paper-bags made from school-books or business letters—collected up as waste-paper from houses and offices by hawkers and resold. Built up in the shape of pyramids with wooden crates for market-sellers to stand on, were baskets of carrots, cabbages, tomatoes, cucumbers, beetroots, chillies, pineapples, beans, tapioca roots, onions, garlic bulbs and dried shrimps.

At one table lay plucked chickens, pale and shining, with yellow legs—round chopping blocks beside them; at another flabby chunks of pork fat hung suspended from wires; at a third fish lay wriggling on banana leaves. Outside in the narrow lane girls and women would squat beside flat round baskets with chillies, limes, fish or shrimps. Booths on each side, protected by sunshades jutting out on poles, offered garlands of sweet-scented flowers and, according to season, mangoes, mango-steens, durians, pomelos, papayas, rambutans and fruits with no European name. . . .

In shops foods vary considerably. Some, like tinned fruit, jams and biscuits, are expensive, with a heavy duty added. Staple imports are tinned milk and flour and for the household, textiles and kerosene. Consumption is 'capricious', states Dr James Ingram in his valuable survey *Economic Change in Thailand since 1850*, and since there is no set pattern of buying, stores have to carry a wide range of novelties to attract custom. A large number of people, especially in the North and North-East, buy no imported goods at all.

CLOTHING

Thais now have virtually no national dress. Unlike Indians, Burmese, Malays and Vietnamese, middle-class Thais, both men and women, wear European clothes. During Pibun's nationalistic phase, all Thais, whatever their status, were ordered to wear shoes and hats, and policemen had to enforce this; it was considered backward and uncultured not to resemble Europeans. To some extent this attitude still exists. Modern Thais are hurt when foreigners admire the naked children running around and try to photograph them. Nudity, they feel, does not accord with progress.

Whereas older women still favour the *panung*—worn like the Indian *dhoti*—as do men on formal occasions, most women, except the middle classes, have adopted the northern *pasin*—a tubular skirt reaching to the ankles and wrapped around like a sarong. This is worn with a blouse, either outside or tucked in, and sometimes no blouse. Men invariably wear shorts or trousers at work, while at home they put on *pakaoma*, their wide checked cloth, or Chinese trousers. The Chinese, men and women alike, also wear these silky trousers; working women sometimes appear in *samfoo* (a flower-patterned pyjama set) but only the wealthy can afford the *cheongsam*, Cantonese style, slit at the sides.

Dress for mourning was once white garments, and heads were shaven; now women wear black at the cremation ceremony, and men white suits, with black tie and armband. A period of mourning is customary, sometimes lasting several months in the case of rich or noble families. As well as school uniforms another adaptation from the West is the holiday-wear of girls and young women—tight-fitting, gaily-coloured jeans, which meet Thai requirements both of modesty (not exposing the legs) and elegance.

HOUSES

Most Thais still live in wooden houses, or up-country, in bamboo or leaf huts. The simplest houses consist of a platform, raised on stakes about six feet above the ground, and divided into two or three rooms and a verandah, with walls of plaited bamboo and a roof thatched with palm leaves. An outside ladder or staircase, with stairs of uneven number to prevent spirits entering, leads to the verandah or direct to the main room. Women and children sit at the entrance much of the day, simply watching and waiting.

Houses built in this way are to be found almost everywhere in Thailand, in town and country alike. During the rainy season the ground may be flooded for several months. In the dry season (November to May) pigs or chickens may live under rural houses; when it rains they perch on mounds of earth. Buffaloes can often be seen huddled on these islands, surrounded by water, sometimes with a roof over their heads.

Town houses are built according to the same plan, but raised on concrete or earth foundations. The main room is simply repeated on the first floor and other rooms added as need arises. In wooden houses, walls are not built quite up to the level of the ceiling so as to leave space for air. These houses are built of unvarnished teak, attractive when new, but they degenerate to a dull and dusty grey.

A typical example of the simplest form of house is that of a bus driver and his family who drove piles into a small canal, built their platform on top, hammered in planks for walls and fitted a corrugated-iron roof. This tiny space for many months was where the whole family cooked, ate and slept. After a time they drove more piles into the mud to support an extension, open on three sides. Finally they erected another platform, partly walled it in and added a roof. A further extension was made for their charcoal stove.

Electric light is tapped from neighbours but there is no water supply. Water has to be fetched in kerosene cans for washing and cooking, and rain is collected when it comes. Their lavatory is the stream.

At breakfast-time the women take turns to cook the rice, squatting in their long cotton skirts by the stove. Baskets, pots and saucepans hang on the walls, others lie drying on packing-case tables. Seven people, sometimes more, live in this hut: two women, the husband of one (the other's husband, the original builder, has left her for his first wife), a grown-up son, three small children and a baby in its hammock.

Conditions are simple: there is fresh air, constant fresh water and the husband has his daily work. It is humid most of the time and warm; only around January is it necessary to put on more than a shirt and trousers—or use a blanket at night. Rice and fish are abundant, though not always cheap.

Possessions are few: mats and pillows to sleep on (the mats are rolled up in the day-time), pots and pans, baskets, a movable charcoal stove no bigger than a bucket, a few clothes hung up on nails, a big shanghai water-jar, mosquito nets, if they are not too expensive for the peasants to buy, and perhaps a gold belt or necklace to wear.

'When a family wish to build a new house,' wrote Mgr Pallegoix in his *Description du Royaume Thai ou Siam* a hundred years ago—and it is the same today over much of the country—'they procure all the materials necessary, then invite all their relatives and friends; at the appointed day the people arrive, armed with picks, sickles, knives, axes, saws and chisels; some dig holes for the posts, others split bamboos; the former prepare the posts, the latter the frame. . . . The family they work for are completely engaged in cooking, preparing cigars, areca and betel, serving tea, cakes and arak (palm-spirit); all the workers, squatting or sitting on mats, eat together . . . ; afterwards they return to work and before the end of the day the house is ready as if by magic.'

Village co-operation still serves for simple bamboo huts, but teak houses have to be built by skilled carpenters, usually Chinese. A small wooden house, carpenter-built, costs at least 6,000 baht (£100 or nearly $300), including 1,200 baht (£20, $60) for labour, in the North; it would be much more in the Centre (*Village Life in Modern Thailand* by John E. de Young).

One great danger, with wooden houses, is fire—caused perhaps by a lighted match or cigarette, by a drunkard over-turning a kerosene lamp, a mosquito-net going up in flames, or by burning incense sticks or through faulty electric wires. Fires often ravage the poorer quarters; a five-hour flare in Rajburi, in April 1960, destroyed over two hundred buildings, causing damage estimated at ten million baht. A fire at Chachoengsao next month burned three hundred houses, leaving over two thousand homeless. Strong winds fanned the fire and the one fire engine in the province was powerless against the blaze. Fires break out every dry season. A disastrous fire in Bangkok, in October 1960 burned down over six hundred wooden shanties in a slum district, causing thirty million baht damage and leaving three thousand people—mostly Chinese labourers —destitute. Since then huge fires have occurred at Ubon, Surind and Pitsanulok and again in Bangkok.

Wooden houses are still found in clusters throughout Bangkok—along railway lines, off commercial roads and even in residential areas—but modern brick and concrete houses, in their own compounds, are rapidly increasing in number. Two or three-bedroomed houses, especially for foreigners, rent from 2,000 baht to 6,000 baht (roughly £30 to £100; $100 to $300) a month. Careful landlords make out two contracts: one for the house, on which they pay tax; and one—of equal amount, or more—for the furniture, on which they don't. The cost of land is now very high. Near the centre of Bangkok, but just off the roads, land may cost 40,000 baht a *rai* (over £1,600— $5,000— an acre) and 10,000 baht two or three miles away. At Pataya, the new seaside resort for wealthy Thais with its villas, yacht clubs, water-ski-ing and so on, land costs as much as 100,000 baht a *rai*; in the country, away from the towns, it sells at perhaps 80 baht a *rai*. The rich invest in gold and jewellery to show off their wealth and in land, house-renting and money-lending for quick returns: there is little left for industry.

A public housing programme has existed since 1948 but, as a mission from the International Bank reports, planning is 'haphazard'. New housing is going up on the fringes of Bangkok, but the crowded slums in the centre remain untouched; nor does the housing programme fit into the broader plans of the Bangkok Planning Commission. 'As so often in Thailand,' they observe, 'one agency of government seems not to have known or cared about the intentions of another.'

HEALTH

Despite personal cleanliness, the greatest danger to health in Thailand is the dirt which results from over-crowding, poverty and ignorance. Half the population of Thailand, it is estimated, suffer from intestinal diseases. Six out of every ten diseases, Dr Haynal, head of the American Public Health Division (us Operations Mission to Thailand), stated in 1958, were 'filth-borne' diseases—diarrhoea, dysentery, worms and cholera. Cholera, thought to have been eradicated in 1951, broke out seven years later causing 10,000 cases and 1,500 deaths in two months. Every day in Bangkok you could hear the melancholy siren of the ambulance bringing victims to the hospital. Entire villages were evacuated for fear of cholera, causing a break-down in some areas of the whole economy. Eighty per cent of the cholera victims, another American doctor reported later, earned below 400 baht (under £7, $20) a month. Many of these were squatters, who lived in home-made shacks along the banks of canals and whose excreta, carried by the water, infected other parts of the city.

There has been considerable progress in eradicating malaria, smallpox and plague; there have been few cases of smallpox and none of plague since 1952. Malaria, once widespread, is being rapidly overcome. 'In the thickly-forested mountains,' Mgr Pallegoix wrote last century, 'there are fevers so harmful that it is often enough for a traveller to spend one night for him to be attacked by a mortal illness, which they call jungle fever.' As recently as 1943, over 57,000 people in Thailand died of malaria, while five million—a quarter of the population—were sick with the disease. In 1959 ten thousand people died from malaria and half a million were sick. For every one who dies at least a hundred survive. 'Unfortunately,' Dr Haynal observes, 'many survivors remain only partially alive. Repeated malaria infections drain the physical and mental energy of the people.'

The World Health Organization reported in April 1960: 'In Thailand, it has been estimated that fifty million agricultural worker/days were lost each year on account of malaria. This equals a rice harvest of 15,000,000 dollars. . . .'*

Like malaria, many of the intestinal diseases become chronic, Dr Haynal says. 'Their victims are neither sick nor well, their energy and vitality slowly being sapped.' Yet these diseases can easily be controlled if people do three things: drink only pure water from protected sources; use sanitary latrines; keep their dwellings clean and stop flies from breeding.

Unfortunately it is the poorest parts of the country which show the most ignorance and the greatest reluctance to change their ways. The Thai Director of the Village Health and Sanitation Project spoke of health workers starting full of enthusiasm; 'then they realize their message may be disregarded, that people will just continue in their old ways without paying the slightest bit of attention.' He added: 'You can't imagine the resistance which we encounter in some isolated villages simply because people don't understand what we are trying to do.'

'Leprosy, yaws, rabies, diarrhoeal diseases and dysenteries, intestinal parasites and venereal diseases are still rather widespread in the country and tuberculosis is a continuing problem,' states the International Bank mission, in *A Public Development Program for Thailand*. Substantial progress has been achieved

* Malaria is more devastating than any other disease in the world, the WHO reports. Every year a hundred and fifty million are sick and one and a half million die.

against yaws (prevalent in half the provinces) and there is a pilot project to control leprosy, but 'very little' has been done to prevent the other diseases. Tuberculosis is particularly serious in Bangkok. Obvious limitations are the 'basic deficiencies of sanitation and housing facilities'.

But health services, the mission's report continues, have improved considerably in the past ten years. The number of doctors has doubled, from one to every 13,000 people in 1947 to one to 7,000 in 1956, or about 3,400 doctors in all. As might be expected, most prefer city life and its remunerations—there is one doctor to just over one thousand inhabitants of Bangkok compared to one to thirty thousand up-country. Two-thirds of the nurses, about 5,000 in all, also work in the Bangkok area, though 25,000 more are needed.

Shortages such as these, entailing lack of prevention and cure, undermine the working capacity of the people. As in India and the Middle East the chronic display of idleness is often not idleness at all. The diseased and under-nourished body cannot cope with more than a few hours of work a day.

LABOUR

Thailand is essentially a rural society. Eighty per cent of the people depend on agriculture. 'The workers in the fields are robust and hardened to fatigue,' wrote Mgr Pallegoix, 'they have much to suffer during the five or six months of their labour, but afterwards they are well compensated and spend the other six months of the year in games, festivals and all sorts of amusements.'

Today, agriculture still accounts for almost half the national income and for 85 to 90 per cent of exports. Manufacture, by contrast, amounts for about 12 per cent of the gross national product; the few large plants in existence produce chiefly cement, tobacco, tin, sugar, spirits, beer, paper, soap and textiles. Less than a tenth of the working population is in industry and few firms employ more than fifty workers apiece.

Rice farming still occupies more than 70 per cent of the cultivated area, and produces 40 per cent of the total value of agricultural output. Nearly all the land (80 per cent) is owned by small, independent farmers. After the abolition of slavery, in 1905, freed men sought their own land. It was cheap to set up in farming, states Ingram in *Economic Change in Thailand since 1850*. The Land Act of 1908 gave people the right to own as much land as they could turn to profit (from 20 to 50 *rai*, or 8 to 20 acres). After satisfying their own needs, a family of five could produce enough to pay back in one good year their entire capital expenditure on seeds, tools and buffaloes.

As more land was opened up for cultivation, including poorer land, yields decreased, particularly in the North-East, Thailand's 'depressed' area. Most of the farm area in the North-East is under rice but the yield is just over three-quarters of the average for Thailand. The North-East contains nearly half of the land area of the country and nearly two-fifths of the population, about nine million people. With the same amount of land under rice, the Central Plain produces over half the total crop for the country, the North-East under a third. Normal production for the whole of Thailand is seven to eight million metric tons depending on the weather, of which one to one and a half million are exported. In the North and North-East the

FARM SURVEY (1953)

	North-East	All Thailand
Rice yield (kilograms per *rai*)	197	261
Average cash income (baht per family)	2,093	3,905
Farming days in the year	83	100

farmer and his family still supplement their normal work in the fields by weaving and other handicrafts, but over most of the country—and indeed over Asia as a whole—cottage industries have been ruined by the influx of cheap Western goods.

The Thai farmer waits for the first rains in May or early June to prepare his fields for sowing; five or six weeks later he and his family transplant the seedlings, bundle by bundle, from their special bed to the fields. A working party of thirty-five peasants, according to de Young, can transplant fifteen paddy fields— nearly five acres—in two and a half hours. Seedlings planted, they wait another four or five months, occasionally weeding the fields and tending to the dikes, for the dry season and harvest time. The women and girls may sell produce at the local market; the children watch the buffalo, fish, hunt crabs or prepare palm leaves for roofing. By New Year it is time for threshing, storing and finally selling the rice to Chinese paddy merchants. About half the price of rice at export rates goes to pay the miller, the exporter and the middleman.

'Industrial' labour in the past was provided by the *corvée*— three or four months' compulsory work a year. Peasants were employed building fortresses, temples or palaces, digging canals, making dikes, roads, houses and all royal and public works. Nowadays (the *corvée* was abolished in 1891) much of the labour force is Chinese.

Dr William G. Skinner in his fine study, *Chinese Society in Thailand*, estimates that there are in Bangkok some 54,000 Chinese artisans, a quarter of them women, and about 21,000 Thai, nearly half women. The figure for unskilled labour (in 1955) stands at 38,000 Chinese, including 4,000 women, and 35,000 Thais, including more than 7,000 women.*

'Chinese' here includes 'ethnic' Chinese, that is to say those who habitually speak Chinese and follow Chinese customs, even if they were born in Thailand and are technically Thai nationals. About one-third of all Thai nationals in Bangkok, Skinner considers, are 'ethnic' Chinese. The total number of Chinese in Thailand ('ethnic' and 'alien', i.e. born in China) is now about three million. Nearly half live in and around Bangkok—the business area is almost entirely Chinese—and in the towns of the Central Plain and in the rubber-planting and tin-mining areas of the South. In fact there are more Chinese in Thailand than in Malaya or any other country of South-East Asia.

Thousands of Chinese workers, Skinner writes, built the railway lines extending from Bangkok early this century. From 1870 onwards there was a heavy demand for Chinese building and construction workers, dockers, rice and saw-mill workers, and workers on the roads and in shops and offices. The Chinese labourer, because of the habitual shortage of workers in Thai-

* The 1960 census for Bangkok (1½ million population) excluding Thonburi (½ million) records 113,000 male 'craftsmen, production process workers and labourers' (i.e. both Chinese and Thai) and 44,000 female. Increasing this by one quarter (to account for workers in Thonburi) would indicate nearly 200,000 in all, an increase of 5 per cent a year since 1955.

land (Thais prefer to remain farmers or to work for the government), earned twice as much as he could in Southern China.

Once in Thailand there was a systematic rise in status, from pedlar to stall keeper, from shop assistant to shop owner, from apprentice to manager; the labourer became a foreman, the petty trader a merchant. Skinner relates the fortunes of the founder of a well-known company, who worked as a cook, rice polisher, sampan ferryman and market gardener; he lent out his savings, started a small export business, married into a Thai family, became friendly with the provincial Governor and secured a teak forest concession. He was the 'sub-farmer' (i.e. concessionnaire under the state monopoly) of three gambling houses and by 1910 his company owned five rice mills, a saw-mill and a dockyard.

With the rise of Thai nationalism in the 'thirties, repressive action was taken against Chinese education; secondary schools were closed and language teaching in the primary schools restricted to five or six hours a week; and Chinese business activities were also discriminated against. 'Aliens' were excluded, after the war, from the manufacture of lacquer and niello-ware, from forestry, charcoal selling, hair-cutting, from driving samlors, taxis or buses and from rice cultivation and salt-making.

The Ministry of the Interior proposed in 1958 that further occupations should be reserved for Thai nationals, such as the manufacture of monks' bowls and Buddhist altars, Thai-style sculpture and carving, hand-weaving, brick-making, bamboo and rattan furniture, fruit gardening and the 'operation of boats on the river and canals'. In August 1959 newspapers reported the arrest of seventeen Chinese barbers, eight niello-ware craftsmen and three Thai-language compositors. Thai newspapers fulminate, every so often, against 'unjust means of monopolizing trade'. Through various trade associations, they complain, 'Chinese merchants have taken control of the market completely . . .' It is to be noted that the most vehement detractors of the Chinese are usually themselves of Chinese origin.

CHAPTER 3

IDEAS AND INFLUENCES

—❊❀❊❊—

Materialists hold that the 'ideological superstructure', in other words political theory, philosophy, religion and the arts, only reflects, or distorts, the underlying reality; for Marxists, this means the 'relations of production'.

If the ideology has obvious links with material conditions, as for example when the 'Promoters' in Thailand—the rising young officers and officials, excluded from preferment—decided to put an end to absolute monarchy, then it 'reflects' these conditions; if not, it 'distorts'. Idealists, on the other hand, believe in the primal Idea, which pervades and informs the whole working of society. In both cases, only one or two, or a few, 'know' what is real (or ideal) and so are in harmony with the rhythm of production (or the universe); the rest, unwittingly, play their pre-ordained part.

Communism, curiously, is a mixture of both. Objectively, Communists cannot gain power until material conditions are ripe; when the outworn relations of production become 'fetters' on production, or more simply, when capital is concentrated into fewer and fewer hands at the expense of everyone else, ex-capitalists included. The latter are all transformed into a downtrodden proletariat, on the verge of revolt, with 'nothing to lose but their chains'. In theory, in other words, Communism is the inevitable result of the fatal over-development of industrialized societies. Yet Communists have never gained control of such industrialized countries: the reverse is true. When they seized power in Russia and China they had to industrialize rapidly; this made the facts fit the theory.

The 'Idea' of Communism held by Communists therefore plays a considerable part in the actual development of Communist society and, of course, among sympathizers in non-Communist countries. It may not be fanciful to attribute an equal importance to religion, whenever belief is strongly held.

Cycles and
Samlors

Elephant hauling
logs

Country bus

2

Canal life

Bangkok shop

Boats at
Ayuthaya

It is often suggested that one of the decisive events of South-East Asia in the last thousand years—the downfall of the great Khmer Empire—was due to the exhaustion of its citizens from fighting incessant wars and building ever greater temples and palaces, the consequent neglect of irrigation on which the food supply depended, but in particular to the vital change in religion which affected both King and people.

GOD KINGS

In common with other peoples of this region some fifteen hundred years ago the Khmers (Cambodians) had absorbed Hindu religions and royal customs. Besides worshipping Vishnu and Shiva, of whom their kings were considered reincarnations, the Khmers accepted Mahayana Buddhism—the more elaborate, expansive Buddhism of China, Tibet and Japan. This form of Buddhism was also pressed into the service of the royal cult. The kings were 'Boddhisatvas'—future Buddhas whose grace won salvation not just for themselves but for all humanity. As they ruled on earth, so in their divine state they ruled in heaven.

The cult of the god-king, Georges Coedès explains in his excellent account *Pour mieux comprendre Angkor*, was carried to extraordinary lengths. In erecting an image of the 'lord of the Universe', the Khmers believed they were fixing for ever in the stone the very essence of the person they wished to adore. No image, according to ancient Indian ideas, could be the object of a cult unless it was 'living'—that is to say animated by the believed presence of the god.

Entire temples were consecrated to the king or his relatives who, on their deaths, became Vishnu, Shiva or Buddha. Each temple was thus a tomb, a kind of artificial body, Coedès says, designed to shelter the image in the way the human body shelters the soul. The same conception is to be found in the *Chedis*, or *Stupas* of Cambodia and Thailand, built even today over the ashes of kings and princes. The Khmer kings took extraordinary care to assure the cult of their images by continuous prayer and worship. A royal inscription reads: 'This supplication I offer to the prosperity of my foundation,

D

this supplication is the immortality to which one should aspire.'

The image, originally a *lingam* or phallus, stood within the temple placed in the very centre of the royal city; the city itself represented the ideal centre of the world. At the summit of the temple the king, through the intermediary of the consecrated image, entered into relation with the divine world. Suryavarman II, founder of Angkor Wat in the early twelfth century, was buried in this mausoleum, which was decorated with *aspara* (celestial dancers) to represent Vishnu in his palace.

The broad moat and the great walls of Angkor further symbolized the seven circular mountains and eight oceans surrounding Mount Mehru, abode of the gods. In Thailand the 'Phra Meru'* had the same significance as the site of the royal cremation ground in the heart of Bangkok—but since 1932 it has become a public park and even, for a short time, the 'Hyde Park' of Thai orators. The walls of Angkor stand, but they failed to preserve that harmony with the universe to which the kings aspired, or rather, the gentle influence of orthodox Theravada Buddhism, spreading from Ceylon throughout present Burma and Thailand, undermined the powerful fantasies of the Khmers. Acknowledging the Buddhist precepts of poverty, peace and detachment from the self, the Khmers, in Coedès's phrase, laid down the crushing burden of glory.

BUDDHISM

Pleasure and grandeur are illusions, the Buddhist holds, for nothing is permanent. To every man comes sickness, old age and death, repeated over and over again; the world 'grows old and dies only to be reborn and grow old and die again and again without cease'. The life of man is pain: 'birth is pain, old age is pain, sickness is pain, death is pain, union with unpleasant things is pain, separation from pleasant things is pain, not getting what one wishes and pursues is pain; the body is

---

* *Phra Meru*, according to transliteration, but it is pronounced *Phramane*. The written Thai preserves the original Sanskrit.

pain, feeling is pain, the mental elements are pain, consciousness is pain. . . .'*

'Craving' is the cause of pain; craving for what one cannot
get, or if one can, for what will not last. Only renunciation can
end that pain: 'the complete and trackless destruction, cessation,
abandonment, relinquishment and rejection of that craving'.
All forms of pleasure, every attachment in the world, must be
discarded: such forms are 'recognized by the eye, desirable,
agreeable, pleasing, attractive, rousing passion and exciting'.
These are 'fetters' equally of ignorance and selfishness, which
bind one to the world and so, inevitably, to old age, sickness
and death.

So also with 'sounds recognized by the ear, scents recognized
by smell, tastes recognized by the tongue, tangible things
recognized by the body and mental things recognized by the
mind, desirable, agreeable, pleasing, attractive, rousing passion
and exciting'. Only through freedom from 'passion' can the
disciple find release. The 'fire of life' must be put out. *Nirvana*
is the extinction of the flame.

Subduing all forms of attachment, the disciple attains the
first 'trance' of meditation, which is 'free from sensual desire
and wicked and evil ideas, is accompanied with reasoning and
investigation, arising from seclusion, and full of joy and
pleasure'. The second trance is 'without reasoning and investigation, arises from concentration, and is filled with joy and
pleasure'. The third is 'without joy', with equanimity towards
joy and aversion. The fourth is the abandonment of both
pleasure and pain, 'mindfulness purified from pain and
pleasure'.

This is enlightenment (the Buddha is the 'enlightened one')
symbolized by the image of the Buddha in the 'lotus posture',
one hand cupped in the lap, the other pointing to the earth.
The lotus, most beautiful of flowers, opens its petals above the
waters; it signifies purity rising from the material world. The
Buddha is seated on a lotus throne, an indefinable expression of
serenity on his face. The artists of the Khmer Empire and the
first Thai kingdoms have captured in sandstone and bronze the

* These and other quotations are from: *The road to Nirvana* by E. J. Thomas;
Buddha and Buddhism by Maurice Percheron; and *Buddhism* by Christmas Humphreys.

essence of compassion and peace which Buddhism brings to them.

This is the end of the Way, but the Way is open to all. 'Cease to do evil; learn to do good; cleanse your own heart' goes the Pali canon. (Sanskrit was the cultural language of the Hinduized kingdoms of South-East Asia, Pali the religious.) Buddhism provides five moral precepts for all men: refrain from taking life; give freely, but take nothing that is not given; never lie; avoid drugs and drink; refrain from unnatural lusts.

These five precepts have had immense significance wherever Buddhism is observed. Gentleness, generosity and peacefulness are characteristic virtues of Buddhist peoples. They have not prevented wars, of course, any more than Christianity has done, but at least there have never been Buddhist wars—or persecutions either. The Thai people are still reluctant to take life— whether of political opponents or of animals and insects. Thais also 'value frankness and sincerity', states Mgr Pallegoix, 'though this is not to say that lies are unknown; on the contrary, they often lie, but rarely to their equals; they nearly always lie to their superiors in order to escape a threatened punishment.'

The French bishop paints a delightful picture of the Thai character before the modern era. In itself it is something of a tribute to Buddhist influence, for the Thais were by no means originally 'soft, light . . . timid'. The Thais, he says—

'do not like disputes or anything which arouses anger or impatience; they would be scandalized to hear a priest speaking with zeal and vehemence. They are lazy, unstable, forgetful . . . They never let a poor man go by without giving him cowries, rice or fruits . . . The Thais are great lovers of games and amusements, and they spend almost half their life in enjoyment. They are witty and intelligent and very well imitate certain artistic objects from Europe . . .

'The nation is notable for its gentleness and humanity; in the capital, which is highly populated, there are rarely serious disputes; a murder is regarded as a most extraordinary event and sometimes the whole year passes without one [this is far from true today].

'The Thais receive strangers with benevolence; they are

most zealous in providing for travellers; at their own cost, private persons build brick paths and wooden bridges and at various places they put up shelters along the river where travellers can halt, cook and spend the night.'

(Even today the average Thai family gives several hundred baht a year for the upkeep of village wats and food for the monks.)

Buddhism encourages the laity to adopt those 'good manners' which are so conspicuous and welcome today. For the monk—and none can achieve *nirvana* without passing through the stage of priesthood—there are stricter rules and observances, over two hundred in all, recited before the community twice a month. Most important of these are, as in Christian orders, poverty, celibacy and non-violence. The outstanding difference is the 'voluntary principle'. There are no permanent vows for the Buddhist priesthood, nor indeed is there a priesthood or Church in the Christian sense at all. Any monk can return to the world at will. Every man is in fact encouraged to become a monk, usually for three months, at least once in his life, usually as a young man before marriage. The government and the armed services give special leave with pay to those entering the monastery. 'Kindly forgive all the wrong done to you by him', the young entrant appeals, 'for the sake of the purity of his priesthood.'

Monks are greatly respected: in Thailand they are known as *phra*, the word for royal or sacred. In a country where in the past anyone who did not prostrate himself before the king faced death, the king himself would bow to a monk. There are good monks and bad monks, inevitably, among the great number (nearly 200,000) who live in some 21,000 monasteries in Thailand. Some monks are idle, some indulge in intrigue, though not as much as certain political monks in Burma or Ceylon, and some are ignorant and superstitious.

W. A. Graham, nearly forty years ago, writes sceptically of Thai Buddhist meditation: 'A number of Pali formulae, learnt by heart, are repeated to assist this meditation, and it is probable that the mechanical muttering over and over again of a string of meaningless words in a half-understood language is, in effect, a powerful aid to the inducement of that foggy and bemused state of mind which is said to be the right condition for the reception of divine illumination.'

This can equally apply nearer home; in fact the whole question of comparing religions (or politics) is bedevilled by the confusion between theory and practice. Early Christian missionaries to the East criticized the ignorance and super-stition of Buddhist monks and drew up elaborate reports on the strange and varied hierarchies of spirits and angels which infested the oriental atmosphere. Not only did they overlook similar beliefs held by themselves or their followers ('Revela-tions' has as much to offer as Thai cosmology), but they ignored the fact that these are of Brahmin origin, repudiated or ignored by the Buddha. Superstition is indeed prevalent in the East, as among all rural peoples, but learned monks and abbots have no part in it.

Buddhism in its pure form is a sublime and noble creation totally distinct from, and indeed opposed to, reliance on ritual as a means of salvation. It is not faith, the Buddhist considers, but following the way the Buddha prescribes that leads to *nirvana*. 'Betake yourself to no external refuge' are his words. 'Hold fast as a refuge to the truth. Look not for refuge to anyone besides yourself. Work out your own salvation with diligence.'

Buddhism is the most reasonable of religions—the Buddha is a great and good man, neither God nor prophet—yet it rests on assumptions which must be taken on trust. These are that rein-carnation indeed occurs, and that as a man sows so shall he reap; that according to his acts and intentions, good or bad, so his 'destiny' (*karma*) works out in this and future lives. Poor men or unhappy men are thus responsible, by their past mis-deeds, for their present condition; yet by doing good they may rise again and, by an absolute detachment, finally attain *nirvana*.

Though Buddhism is the 'Middle Way' between the extremes of asceticism and ritual—which are either misleading or meaningless—it reveals essentially a revulsion against the world. Unlike Christianity it is individual, not social; negative (the extinction of passion or delight), not positive (love of God and of one's neighbour). Yet the Buddhist layman can echo the Christian precepts of compassion and love; and the Christian contemplative, in silence and meditation, is not far removed from the Buddhist way.*

BRAHMINISM

The religion of the Buddha was a reaction against the excessive Hindu ritual ordained by Brahmin priests and equally against the view that these mysteries—as with Communism and the Commissars—could only be known, and practised, by the elect. Buddhism, on the contrary, was open to all. But while the orthodox Buddhist religion was brought by the Thais to the Khmer Empire (with the results we have seen), the Thais in return adopted Brahminical rites to sanctify their own newly-established kings.

Brahminism to this day is the conduct of court ceremony, designed to assure the supposed harmony of the monarch with the divine order, and thus the prosperity of the realm; on this Buddhism, rightly, had nothing to say. Similarly with marriage: marriage is a natural state and even, as such, a 'fetter' to that detachment from worldly things to which the Buddhist aspires. So if a marriage is celebrated at all, which is not strictly necessary, the actual rites are Brahminical rites. Again with popular festivals—those opportunities for amusement which the Thais so much enjoy—most are of Brahminical origin, except for certain religious ceremonies commemorating notably the Buddha's first sermon at Benares and the day of his birth, enlightenment and death.

The *Songkran*, or Water Festival, is the manifestation of Phra In (Indra), lord of the lower heavens, descending to earth. 'If he rides upon a *Nak* dragon,' Graham explains, 'it is a sign of rain; if upon a *Khrut* bird winds will be high; a cow or buffalo as steed presages agricultural prosperity.' There is a vigorous

* Strictly the Buddhist considers that (1) everything has a cause and every cause must have an effect, at some time or another. Good causes have good effects, and *vice versa*, but the effects are not always produced in one life-time. (2) It is not the soul that is transmitted to another life or lives but these effects, good or bad. Belief in the soul, or self, or personality, is an illusion. The 'self' is merely an 'aggregate' of the faculties of touch, sight, consciousness, etc. which are subject to change (from cause and effect) like everything else. (3) Buddhism is not the search for goodness or happiness, which is also an illusion, but the search for truth. He who knows the truth has found enlightenment.

outpouring of water, 'that libation to the earth in spring which is amongst the oldest and most widely practised ceremonies of propitiation in the world.' The *Nak* (Sanskrit Naga) is the mythical serpent, guardian of temples: a Naga princess was legendary ancestor to the Khmer Empire and it was the king of the Nagas who by tradition protected the Buddha after his enlightenment. The *Khrut* (Garuda) is the mount of Vishnu and the emblem of government in Thailand. Nagas and Garudas are as known and accepted in the Hinduized East as are Lions and Unicorns in the West.

The God Shiva (Phra Isuen or Iswara in Thai) appears in the ancient swing ceremony of Bangkok which, because of numerous accidents, has not been held for many years. But the first ploughing ceremony, exceedingly ancient, has recently been revived by Marshal Sarit. On the first occasion the bulls, frightened by enormous crowds, broke loose and the auspicious plough had to be drawn by government officials. A recaptured bull, invited to choose between various offerings, took liquor. Brahmins interpreted this, correctly no doubt, as indicating an expansion of tourism in Thailand because foreigners like whisky!

White elephants are of particular significance in Brahminical lore as their possession guaranteed power and prosperity to the King and his people. Major wars have been fought between Burmese and Thais over these beneficent beasts. Not long ago a baby white elephant was found in the forest and trained at the Bangkok Zoo. According to the announcement of the dedication ceremony (November 1959) 'a chapter of twenty high-ranking monks will chant prayers while gongs, conch-shells and drums are sounded.' The King and Queen present yellow robes and white bags to the monks, light candles and joss sticks and receive blessings. Further candles are lit in worship of *devada* (Hindu gods): Brahminical rites follow. Next day 'as the Royal Astrologer sounds a gong to announce the auspicious hour, the King will mount a platform, pour lustral water on the elephant and climb down.

'He will anoint a piece of red sugar-cane and write on it the name to be given to the elephant. The name is Phra Savet Adulyadej Brahana. The Chief of Brahmins will then conduct Brahminical rites. The King will present ceremonial regalia to the elephant. The monks will chant prayers and then retire.

'The Chief of Brahmins will sing a metrical composition to the elephant. A *wien-thien* rite, in which tapers are passed from hand to hand in a circle around the elephant, fanning the smoke towards it, will follow. Conches, trumpets and drums will be sounded.'

Industry, too, is blessed by Brahmins, while 'gongs, conch-shells and drums are sounded'.

GUARDIANS AND SPIRITS

'It is a well-authenticated fact,' Graham states, 'that in many countries of the Far East it was formerly considered necessary, when any royal or national building was to be erected, to bury one or more human bodies, either alive or freshly killed for the purpose, beneath the foundations.' The *San Chao Lak Muang* (Shrine of the lord of the Pillar of the country) is to be found in the ruins of all ancient cities. It is a pillar of wood or stone, considered the symbol of national existence, surrounded by effigies of tutelary deities and guardians.

An image of Brahma, the four-headed god, creator of the world, stands in its own shrine in the compound of the 'Erawan', the government-owned luxury hotel. This is an imposing example of what exists in every Bangkok compound and in every up-country village—the *Phra Phum Chao Thi*—or sacred owner of the land; a propitiation to the lord or spirit of the earth for its use by man. In most households it is a small temple-shaped structure, often in bright colours, mounted on a pillar. Inside is the carved outline of a Hindu god, Thai-style, and in the precincts plaster figures of horses, cattle or slaves promised in return for favours rendered. The spirit is popularly supposed to mistake these toy figures for the real articles. Flowers, incense-sticks, fruit and rice may also be offered; the latter are withdrawn for domestic use after a suitable interval. This is not taken very seriously in Bangkok but the tradition is still followed, no doubt to avoid running any risk of offending the deities.

But in the country the Buddhist religion itself is little more than a veneer on popular beliefs and supernatural fears. The country, Graham points out, is full of the ghosts of people murdered or devoured by wild animals, of women dead in child-birth, men who have died away from home, and sudden victims of cholera, and so on. These ghosts are especially malevolent and difficult to propitiate.

The bite or scratch of some spirits, Graham adds, can cause sickness, which is frequently fatal (these spirits are now rapidly being dispelled by DDT); some spirits lead travellers into the path of wild beasts, or lure them over precipices; some entrance susceptible males by their diabolical beauty and afterwards devour them; some strike death and disease into those who would rob the treasures of caves or temples; and some (known also nearer home) frighten children in the dark.

CHINESE FEATURES

Malevolent spirits in Thailand, and their attributes, are very similar to the Chinese *kuei* (devils), which lurk in ponds and rivers to drown the unwary, bring famine and disease, haunt the graves of suicides, the insane and those who have died in childbirth. *Kuei* are associated, states Dr K. S. Latourette in *The Chinese: their History and Culture*, with the well-known force of *yin*—the earth, moon, darkness, evil, female. The dragon, phoenix and unicorn represent the *yang*—sun, light, fire, goodness, male, though these particular symbols are not observed in Thailand.

The obvious similarity of popular beliefs—including auspicious days for marriages, building or going on a journey, though these are not, of course, peculiar to the Chinese— indicate the origins of the Thai people. The Thai language closely resembles Chinese in its tones, 'classifiers' for nouns and use of monosyllables. Thai, like Chinese, has no gender or inflexions, and verbs are not declined; *Khao pai ban* in Thai (rising, level and falling tones) means he (or it, she or they) goes (or go) to the house. *Khao*, in different tones, also means: rice, white, news, knee, mountain and the verb to enter. Thai numbers are pronounced either identically or akin to the Chinese, especially Cantonese. Family relationships—the use

of separate words to describe maternal or paternal grand-
parents, uncles and aunts, juniors or seniors in age, younger or
older brothers and sisters—are all closely connected.

Traditional Chinese outlook, noted by Latourette, clearly
resembles Thai behaviour: for example, sensitiveness to 'loss of
face', and the consequent avoidance of public humiliation or
injured feelings; dislike of physical violence yet, at the same
time, subjection to sudden spasms of anger; open curiosity
about the age and incomes of others; and the almost universal
indulgence in gambling. 'Every day,' confirms Mgr Pallegoix,
'one sees such passionate gamblers that, having lost all they
have, they end by playing even for the sarong they are wearing.'
Horse-racing or cock-fighting for men, cards for men and
women, beetle or fish fights for children—the national lottery
for everyone—all are turned to account.

Marriage differs in that the Thai (unlike the Chinese) often
returns with his bride to her father's house and may settle in
the same house, or one newly built in the same compound or
nearby. Divorce, which is as simple and easy as most Thai
marriages, is by mutual consent—the property and the children
being evenly divided. 'If a husband and wife have a physical
and mental distaste and desire to be divorced,' states the fourteenth century law (W. A. R. Wood's *History of Siam*), 'let it be
as they wish; for they two have no further blessing on their union,
and therefore should not be compelled to live together.' 'In
general,' Mgr Pallegoix observes, 'Siamese wives are well
treated by their husbands, they have much authority in ruling
the family, they are honoured, they enjoy great freedom. . . .
They appear in public, go to the market, do business, give and
receive visits, walk to pagodas in town and in the country, and
have nothing to fear from the jealousy of their husbands.'

The Chinese practice of taking concubines is related to the
Thai system of *mia noi*, or 'junior wife'. 'Many people have two
wives: the mandarins up to twelve, the princes up to twenty,
thirty, forty and above; and the king numbers them in hundreds,' observed Mgr Pallegoix a hundred years ago.

Note that the Thai word *mia* is used for wife, in this sense, and
not the polite Sanskrit word *phanraya*. Natural and emotional
associations, as opposed to abstract conceptions, are rendered in
Thai rather than Sanskrit (in fact, there are almost no abstract

words in Thai), just as we use Anglo-Saxon rather than words of French or Latin origin in similar circumstances. 'Freedom' means more to us than 'liberty'; in fact *Thai* is the old word for 'free', though what is at present used is the Sanskrit *Seri*: the war-time 'Free Thai' movement, led by Pridi and others, was *Seri Thai*.

But to return to the *mia noi*. She is more than a mistress and less than a wife. It is a compromise for the eastern husband between fidelity on the one hand and promiscuity (though this is not debarred) on the other. The wealthy, and even the not so wealthy, Thais generally support their *mia noi* in separate establishments. Pretty young girls driving their own Fiats or Mercedes may be the *mia noi* of Cabinet Ministers or senior officials, army officers or business men. Thailand's most influential editor, Kukrit Pramoj, once denied that members of the present Government, if not of its predecessor, had gone too far: 'I have not yet heard,' he wrote, 'that any of them had taken schoolgirls, while still studying, to become their wives. At least they are decent enough to wait till they graduate.'

The Thais, too, followed the Chinese system of government by 'mandarinate', or professional body of officials, though never to the extent of a recognized system of examination for entry. It was monopolization of higher posts by the aristocracy in this century—the numerous progeny of King Chulalongkorn and his many wives—that drove the professional element in Thailand to revolt. Hereditary aristocracy, which might overshadow as in Europe the primacy of the king, was prevented in China as in Thailand by an ingenious device. A lower title was passed on to each succeeding generation until they finally reverted to commoners. It is as if the sons of a royal prince in England were all dukes, their grandsons earls, their great-grandsons viscounts and so on, down to barons, baronets and esquires. Highest Thai titles are *chao fa* (royal children), *phra ong chao* (son of the king and another wife) though this is not appropriate today, and *mom chao* (sons of *phra ong chao*). Prince Wan Waityakon, a distinguished, elder statesman (the Talleyrand of Thailand), was born *mom chao*, but has been raised for his services. Then follows *mom rajawong* (sons of princes), as for example Kukrit Pramoj and his brother Seni, a 'Free Thai' leader during the war; *mom luang* (sons of *mom rajawong*) and finally *nai* (plain mister). Official titles (i.e. conferred, not inherited) correspond in grade: *Chao Phya* (the highest honour, as given to the Menam river), *phya*, *phra*, *luang* and *khun*. But all official titles were abolished by Pibun (himself a *luang*) and no more have been given. As the royal titles decline, with the absence for many years of huge royal families, so titles of all sorts in Thailand will become almost extinct.

Since the end of absolute monarchy (1932) there has been no influential aristocracy but an upper-class leadership of Army generals and colonels, senior officials and certain politicians, to whom wealth—a necessary attribute of power—has accrued. The Army, originally in the vanguard of the rising bourgeoisie (as in the Middle East today), has been so long involved in politics, and indeed in business, that it has lost its zeal for reform. No longer under-privileged, it is a pillar of the existing order. It was the Army, under the previous regime, which provided almost all the nominated members of the Assembly (i.e. nearly half the total legislature); Army officers still head various government agencies, manage the Army TV and 'direct' numerous commercial concerns. The absence of an elected Assembly and the continuance of martial law openly confirms today what was previously concealed under democratic forms.

THAI LEADERS

Kings		Prime Ministers	
1767	Tak Sin	1933	Bahon
1782	Rama I	1938	Pibun
1809	Rama II	1944–46	Khuang, Tawee, Seni
1824	Rama III	1946	Pridi
1851	Mongkut	1946–47	Thamrong, Khuang
1868	Chulalongkorn	1948	Pibun
1910	Vajiravud	1957	Pote, Thanom
1925	Prajadhipok	1958	The Revolution
1932	End of Absolute Monarchy	1959	Sarit

CHAPTER 4

A PREVIEW OF POLITICS:
HOME AND ABROAD

Thais are not keen on doing more work than is necessary; their needs are few and are easily supplied. Others less fortunate may call them lazy. Thailand is probably the least intellectually curious country in Asia. One thing, however, is overlooked, and that is the tremendous rise in agricultural production and with it the prosperity of the people.

According to Ingram in *Economic Change in Thailand since 1850*, in less than a hundred years rice exports increased *twenty-five times*, while the population doubled. The Central Plain, from Bangkok to the northern foothills, produced over 95 per cent of these exports (or half the total crop). In the first fifty years, the price itself doubled.

This was the result of foreign demand, stimulated by the use of modern transport—railways, steam ships, the Suez Canal. Just as wheat came under production on a gigantic scale in America, Canada and the Ukraine, so land was reclaimed and irrigated for rice fields and plantations throughout South-East Asia.

King Mongkut himself and his son, the great King Chula-longkorn, actively encouraged this development. No tax was levied on land newly under cultivation for the first three years, Ingram writes, and thereafter only a small tax, estimated at a third or a fifth of the average in the Far East. Land was declared available to all who wished to farm it—at least ten acres a man. Instead of being the preserve of the great land-owners (as in Latin America and the Philippines, the legacy of Spain), the land belonged to sturdy, independent owner-farmers.

Just as the land reforms of the French Revolution had saved nineteenth-century France from civil war (despite uprisings in Paris), so Thailand, almost alone of South-East Asian countries in this century, has been spared insurrection and unrest. Bangkok, like Paris, is an exception. In fact the leaders of the first successful *coup d'etat* were trained in France.

Admittedly Thailand was never a colony—partly through the wisdom and foresight of the two great kings of Siam who, like the Meiji emperors of Japan, adapted their countries to the West; partly because neither Britain nor France could allow the other to seize control. The French during their policy of outright colonial conquest were the worst offenders. While the British took over certain Malay-speaking Thai tributaries in 1909 (Tunku Abdul Rahman, Prime Minister of Malaya, was born under Thai rule), the French had regained four provinces, including the famous Angkor Wat, for Cambodia in 1907 and a large slice along the Mekong (in 1893) for Laos. In that year they had even sent a gunboat up the Menam Chaophraya to threaten Bangkok. The Thais, hoping to restrain it, fitted an iron chain across the river, but it broke.

Thailand was shorn of past conquests but not subdued. Burma and Vietnam, on the other hand, experienced the downfall of the monarchy with all the tremendous psychological shock this involved—for kings bear the mandate of heaven— and the disruption of the established order. Thailand itself was shaken by the coup (1932) which ended absolute monarchy and established a Constitution, or *Rathamanun* ('Who is *Rathamanun*?' the peasants asked).

'Thailand', too, conforming to the customary *Muang Thai*, displaced the royal, Sanskritic 'Siam'. Thai nationalism, in the absence of foreign domination, was conservative rather than revolutionary and, in fact, military rather than civilian. But even Marshal Pibun's ascendancy did nothing to prevent Thailand acquiescing in the Japanese wartime occupation and the 'Greater East Asia Co-Prosperity Sphere'. It was under Japanese auspices that the Thais temporarily regained, from Malaya, Cambodia and Laos, the land they had lost.

But with admirable circumspection—Thais do not believe in unnecessary violence—a 'Free Thai' movement was organized from within the ranks of the rulers. Pridi, then Regent, was their leader: a clandestine leader not for the first, or the last, time. Even before the end of the war, in accordance with permissible expectation, the democrat Pridi had replaced the fascist Pibun—to use wartime terms. But the new civilian administration was unable to cope either with the vast increase of corruption, stemming from the Japanese occupation and consequent inflation, or with the mysterious death of the young king (still not satisfactorily resolved) or, above all, with the undiminished power of the Army. By the outbreak of the cold war, it was the turn of the democrat Pibun to replace the communist Pridi—to use the terminology of the cold war.

This was not just a matter of one face for the rain and another for the sun. Pridi fled in 1947, helped by the British and even, initially, by the Americans: they were a little behind the times. Next year Pibun ousted the caretaker regime of the Democratic leader Khuang: 'I went with bayonets at my back,' he was never tired of repeating. Pridi's followers launched an abortive coup in 1949. Pridi was then in China, which was changing from a Nationalist to a Communist regime. Almost without precedent, politicians, officials and officers were arrested, imprisoned and a number shot 'trying to escape'. Some of Pibun's supporters then fell out and were involved in obscure plots.

There came the fantastic incident of the 1951 'Manhattan affair', when Pibun was kidnapped by a naval officer during the handing-over of a US dredger, taken, under the eyes of the astonished diplomats, on board the Navy flagship, which was then sunk by the Air Force, and had to swim for his life. It was followed by three days of fighting in the streets of Bangkok. Ever since that day, the Navy, supporters of Pridi, have been in disgrace. It is said that even now the fleet has no live ammunition.

That year marked the ascendancy of General Phao, a former assistant to Pibun, ruthless, corrupt but extremely able, and of his rival, Marshal Sarit. Phao, who had been Director-General of the Police since 1948, during which time he successfully liquidated his opponents, became Deputy-Minister of the Interior, and organized a superb opium network. Later he became Secretary-General of the Manangkasila Party and won the general election. Sarit, then commander of the First (Bangkok) Army, became Commander-in-Chief and finally Minister of Defence. All was well until Pibun's world tour, in 1955, when he 'caught' democracy. In the event it was Marshal Sarit who benefited from the removal of controls on the ex-

3

Up-country
store

New Road:
Bangkok

Yawarad Road:
Chinese section,
Bangkok

4   Marble temple

'Marco Polo', Wat Poh   Temple of the Emerald Buddha

pression of public opinion and the formation of political parties, for both Pibun and Phao were discredited by the old system. Disgust with the rigged February 1957 elections brought out the students in protest against Pibun and the opportunism of his pro-Western policies: 'we want democracy, not air-conditioning,' they shouted.* Pibun and Phao were ousted in September that year; Pibun fled to security in Japan, Phao to his securities in Switzerland. (Phao died in November 1960.)

Sarit retained the air-conditioning, provided democracy (for a time), and left his deputy in charge while he underwent a series of operations in America. Barely recovered after being almost a year away—except for one brief visit to stave off, or rather to buy off, support for Khuang's opposition—Marshal Sarit dramatically arrived one day in October 1958 and launched the Revolution. The Constitution was scrapped, the National Assembly dissolved, the political parties disbanded, trade unions ended and martial law put into effect (as it still is today). 'Evils and corrupt practices had multiplied,' stated the leader of the Revolutionary Party. 'Subversion of the government was the order of the day. . . . The National Assembly, the press and certain labour circles had also succumbed (to Communist subversion). Besides, the national economic situation was highly precarious with thousands of millions of baht of debts contracted by the former (Pibun) government. . . .† The garb of democracy was weighing down Thailand. . . . Consequently the Revolutionary Party has to seize power.'

Despite the temptation of arbitrary power, Marshal Sarit has indeed given an impetus to national development, towards progress and away from stagnation. Feared and respected, if not liked, Sarit has chosen Ministers of more integrity and efficiency than those of the past. To appropriate what was once said by another army leader (in the Sudan): Thailand 'is a democratic State and power rests with the people. The head of the high command of the armed forces is the supreme power' in Thailand.

* Cited by David A. Wilson and Herbert J. Phillips in *Far Eastern Survey*, August 1958.

† On the third anniversary of the Revolution (October 20, 1961) Marshal Sarit pointed out: 'The internal confidence in the soundness of our financial situation can be proved beyond any doubt. . . . It is the most important achievement of the Revolutionary Regime in being able to extricate the country from a financial morass.'

E

CHAPTER 5

POLITICS

❧❀❀☙

The parliamentary system, and the Thai parliament building itself, are imports from abroad. The white marble assembly hall, with classical columns, pediments and domes, comes from Italy; the principles aired within from France, Britain and America. But this imposing edifice of democracy, formerly a royal palace, was found too heavy for the shifting soil of Bangkok: to adjust it to the unstable elements, it now rests on adapted 'rafts' of concrete.

First, a word on the Assembly and the Constitution. After 1932, half the members of the Assembly were elected and half nominated. This system of quasi-democracy, considered suitable for a largely illiterate population, was intended to last for ten years, after which time all members would be elected. But Pibun, admittedly in wartime, postponed constitutional change; thus permanent (military) support from the nominated members was assured. Pibun, during his second term in power (1948–57), devised a new Constitution whereby each province was entitled to replace a nominated member by an elected one as soon as it achieved 50 per cent literacy. Pibun continued to hold 'elections' from time to time, but as he could still rely on a substantial number of nominated or 'second category' members, he did not need the votes of many elected members for a majority. Such was the adherence to constitutional proprieties, however, that a majority was always ensured even among the elected members, although the Assembly in fact had little or no control over the Government at all.

The sections which follow discuss the difficulties of inspiring democracy among the mass of the people, describe the abuses of the past regime, the personalities of leading politicians, the background to the Revolution, and the problem of restoring democracy.

AUTHORITY

'Thailand's political system,' consider the editors of the Human Relations Area Files handbook, *Thailand: its people, its society, its culture*, 'is still as underdeveloped as its economy. . . . Just as most farmers work by hand methods for limited economic goals, so do they employ primitive implements in their political life. . . . Both politics and economy lack elaborate organization and systematic ideology.' The first Prime Minister of the constitutional period (who was also Commander-in-Chief) refused to permit political activities; the country, he said, was not ready for party conflict and a legal opposition. Only for three years after the war were parties permitted, but banned again under Pibun up to the time of his world tour; they were allowed briefly to flourish for almost another three years and then under Marshal Sarit abruptly ended.

Civilian rule never effectively developed in these years and elections never aroused popular enthusiasm. Ten per cent of the electorate voted after the overthrow of absolute monarchy, and 20 per cent four years later. Even the post-war civil administration under Pridi attracted no more than 30 per cent of the electorate, and only 40 per cent voted in the first free elections after the fall of Pibun.

Apathy reigns in the countryside, except for the depressed areas of the North-East which vote socialist; villagers vote, if they vote at all, as the headman says. The Government controls the provinces through the Ministry of the Interior; the Ministry appoints governors and district officers, and pays a stipend to the headman. *Kan muang* (politics) means the 'business of the city'; only in Bangkok is politics taken seriously, and then only by a few.

As Bishop Pallegoix pointed out, 'the Siamese are very obedient and show extraordinary respect for authority'. This 'excessive' respect he illustrates by the ceremonial prostrations then required: 'When one goes to see a superior, as soon as he is in sight one must prostrate oneself and worship him, raising one's joined hands above the head, the body bent forward; and one speaks seated, legs behind. . . . Speaking to princes one must say: "I, dust of your august feet, prince who protects my head, I who am the plant under your feet. . . ." (And to the

King) "I, who am a grain of dust under your sacred feet, I receive your orders, divine lord".'

An elaborate ceremonial still symbolizes these hierarchies of respect. In Thai houses the servant creeps past guests with head bowed and serves on his knees. But if he is ill, his master will provide for him till he is cured. A similar 'feudal' relationship pervades Thai political life. The Thai people throughout their history have obeyed their kings and leaders; the latter in turn tend and protect them. Like a father in the family, leaders choose the people they know—i.e. their relatives and friends—for positions of responsibility; they do not rely on an abstract assessment of merit. Personal, paternal, familial—such is the system of rule.

Experience of the past confirms popular acceptance of strong authority; without it, the country has lain exposed to internal dissension or foreign aggression. 'If we look back at our national history,' the present Foreign Minister, Thanat Khoman, has said, 'we can very well see that this country works better and prospers under an authority, not a tyrannical authority, but a unifying authority around which all elements of the nation can rally. On the contrary, the dark pages of our history show that whenever such an authority is lacking and dispersal elements had their play, the nation was plunged into one disaster after another.'

In every country force is the ultimate basis of rule, even if it lies in reserve. But so long as the formal system of government maintains its prestige—assisted in the past by the divine attributes of monarchy—the army serves the 'throne'; only when the latter fails can the army seize command. Yet the instability shown by monarchy as a system of government—given the bloody uncertainties of succession—is no less evident under a military regime. Democracy, though often the rule of mediocrity, at least tries to assure both continuity and change by peaceful means.

Certainly benevolent dictatorship can be better than pseudo-democracy—though the transformation to real democracy may be harder where the forms are lacking. For Thailand the importance of Sarit's ejection of Pibun and Phao, and of his personal assumption of command, is that it marks a break with the past. Not only have the personalities of the Pibun era

(1948–57) been discarded and the arbitrary powers of the police withheld, but Sarit's Revolution, however tentatively, does look forward to national development rather than personal aggrandisement.

PAST EVILS

In South Africa the Minister of Justice once defended the police by saying they had committed no more crimes than anyone else. The police would never have got away with this defence in Thailand during the ten years of the previous regime: they committed a good many more crimes than anyone else.

Corruption, the HRAF Handbook on Thailand states, was probably more highly organized in the Police Department than in any other Department or Ministry. General Phao's political activities were directly financed by the profits from opium smuggling—organized by himself. He maintained virtually an army of police concentrated in Bangkok (for political reasons) and in the North-East, the region of economic discontent. Of a total of some 48,000 police personnel, the handbook reports, about 10,000 were stationed in and around Bangkok, and perhaps 20,000 in the North-East. The Patrol Division of the Metropolitan Police was equipped with armoured cars, tanks and heavy machine guns. Special 'Knights' (*Asawin*) were created for their outstanding services to Phao.*

A storm of criticism burst over Phao the first time people felt free enough to express it, during Pibun's essay in democracy. Early in 1956, at a public meeting on the Phramane Ground—the royal cremation land made into a public park—General Phao swore that he did not know or approve of illegal detention, illegal shooting, the killing of four Cabinet Ministers (in 1949) or the 'gaining of unusual wealth'.

He issued a pamphlet to provincial leaders of the ruling Seri Manangkasila Party to combat criticisms by the Democratic Party. To charges that the Government ruled by *ying-thing* (shooting to kill) and *khang-thing* (illegal detention) the 'answer' was that it ruled by 'democratic methods', while charges of corruption by officials were 'unfair' and charges of 'unusual

* *Thailand, its People, its Society, its Culture*, pages 197–9 ('Police System').

wealth' 'untrue', since 'officials have enough only to live and eat'.

In an outspoken article written after the expulsion of Phao, C. L. Sulzberger of the *New York Times** declared that Phao was a 'sort of local Beria' who did not hesitate to deal with the Communist Chinese themselves, though 'some say this was merely to enlarge his personal fortune'. Phao, he wrote, 'ran the gold exchange and opium trade. He squeezed the Chinese minority. He took a cut on every animal butchered in Bangkok's slaughter-house, which he owned. . . .'

Phao's opium business was well organized. As a Thai newspaper, *Siam Nikorn*, wrote early in 1958: 'It may be recalled that during the director-generalship of Police-General Phao Sriyanond, many high police officers, by availing themselves of the system of giving rewards for capture of illicit opium, were able to amass great riches. They simply flew to the North, found huge stores of opium abandoned by silly smugglers in some forest areas for them to pick up. That was the usual tale told by these Asawin (knight) police officers.

'Actually what the officers did was to send agents to buy illicit opium in North Thailand. When a sizeable stock was obtained, the Asawins came ostensibly to arrest opium smugglers. They got the opium all right, but no opium smugglers could be arrested. The opium was sent down to Bangkok, weighed by the Excise Department and the Asawins reaped the reward based on the current opium price in the capital. It amounted to buying illicit opium for sale at a very good profit to the Government and in this very lucrative trade only the privileged influential class could engage. . . .'

The Democrats accused Phao† not of just printing forged notes in Hong Kong and circulating them in Bangkok, but of amassing 14 million baht (nearly £250,000 or $700,000) of the 27 million baht 'reward' for the seizure of twenty tons of opium. Opium smuggling, the handbook on Thailand states, was virtually a police monopoly. The police operated warehouses, provided a rail-guard and coast-guard escort to Hong Kong, Singapore, Saigon and other outlets. Perhaps three-quarters of the world's supply of opium is grown in Yunnan, South-West China, and distributed via Bangkok.

* November 6, 1957.
† He complained they 'damaged his reputation'.

Local opium smuggling still survives, though the trade has now largely turned to the more dangerous, but less easily detected, sale of heroin. In January 1959 the police (now under new management) searched a bus from Lampang, North Thailand, as it approached Bangkok. They found 147·5 kilograms of opium, valued at 1·2 million baht (£20,000, nearly $60,000), hidden in the roof. 'The opium was kept in flat tins,' the police reported, 'placed on the roof and hidden under strips of timber nailed to the roof tightly enough to appear as part of the roof. The bus was carrying a load of groundnuts.' A large haul of opium—over two tons of it—was also made by the police in November 1960.

In July 1959 the Sarit Government banned legal opium-smoking in Thailand. 'From this day,' the Prime Minister stated, 'we can proudly claim that we are civilized people. . . . I shall have to carry out drastic suppression at all costs, even at the cost of my own life, for I maintain that opium smoking is most injurious to the nation.' (Most opium-smokers are actually Chinese.) Shortly after midnight 8,935 opium pipes, gathered from Government-licensed dens, burned on the Phramane ground.

Under Phao, unlicensed brothels, illegal opium-dens and illicit gambling had all been allowed, provided there were adequate payments to the police. Thugs were hired to threaten Chinese merchants, according to the HRAF handbook (p. 198), to frighten political opponents, to intimidate the press and influence elections. After Pibun's last elections (February 1957), 50,000 illegally-printed ballots were found in Bangkok alone.

The regime certainly deployed all its resources. Phao had predicted they would win 113 of the 160 seats at stake; in fact they won only eighty-three but could count on over 100 'second category', i.e. nominated, members. Whole streets of names were missing from election lists (even Marshal Sarit was at first omitted), *nakleng* (hooligans) were active, and certain Inspection Committee members were bought. 'Paratroopers'—ruffians who cast votes instead of those on the voting list—and 'fire cards'—illegal ballots—were thrown into the fray. General Phao had carefully provided his men with full authority (his instructions were reported later in the Press): 'The holder is helping the police. If there is any arrest, let me know first. Signed Pol. Gen. Phao Sriyanond.'

Buying and selling was the order of the day. Government supporters in the Assembly were paid 2,000 baht (£35, $100) a month in addition to their official salary of 3,650 baht, later increased to 5,650 baht—nearly £100 or $280—a month. In August 1956 the Seri Manangkasila Party gave each of its deputies 5,000 baht and a bale of yellow cloth to organize Buddhist rites for their constituents 'and thus gain their votes'.

Night-clubs were also involved. General Phao denied after the February 1957 elections that there had been a 'fight in Club 85 over competition to obtain places in the new Cabinet'.* He also denied that his party was buying up other deputies at 60,000 baht (£1,000 or nearly $3,000 each). In July 'foreign overthrow' plotters against the government were said to have offered to 'purchase' deputies at 50,000 to 100,000 baht each.

General elections such as these were never intended to express the will of the electorate; they were a convenient device to give the stamp of legality to the group in power. They also served to 'legalize' government by *coup d'état*. The November 1947 *coup*, ousting the administration backed by Pridi, set a precedent for this type of action. 'Public opinion wanted the change,' declared Marshal Pibun (cited in the HRAF handbook), 'and as it could not be done by constitutional means, the former government having a majority in parliament, the Army decided unanimously to get rid of it.'

From violence in getting rid of a government to violence in disposing of political opponents is a short step. Only after Pibun and Phao had fled did relatives of victims who had previously not dared to complain come forward to give evidence of these years of shame.

Two Police Brigadier Generals were convicted of complicity in the murder of four former Cabinet Ministers, near Bangkok, in 1949. Phao's customary excuse for their deaths was that 'an attempt to rescue them was made by Malayan terrorists (near Bangkok!) and they were killed by the terrorists'. The Public

---

* A senior Police Officer was accused early in September of contacts with the Chinese Communists; he was said to have brought 'taxi-dancers' from Shanghai for use in his own night-club. Chinese hostesses, desirably pale, can be a source of political embarrassment.

Prosecutor charged that the defendants used trickery to take the four ex-Ministers, who had been held for investigation after Pridi's abortive *coup*, from police stations in Bangkok to Bangkhen, where they were shot. In September 1959, three defendants were sentenced to life imprisonment and two released for lack of evidence.*

At a 'mass murder' trial held in August 1958, a witness spoke of meeting police officers in the house of a Police Brigadier General, and one of the victims, a deputy from the North-East. A police driver testified that in December 1952 he drove a jeep from Kanchanaburi (west of Bangkok) for nine kilometres along the road and then two kilometres into the forest. A Police Major ordered him to stop. They dug a hole in the ground. Later a large jeep stopped, 'five packets wrapped in mats' were taken to the hole and burned. The Police Brigadier and a Police Colonel were present. Several months later he attended a party at which Police General Phao gave each of them a packet containing money. He was given 30,000 baht (£500 or $1,500).

The Public Prosecution Department, in January 1958, formally charged with murder a Police Lieutenant Colonel and four other policemen. The victim at the time of the murder (March 1953) was Managing Director of the Thai Commercial Company publishing the newspapers *Phim Thai* and *Siam Nikorn*, which had been criticizing the Pibun Government and 'affecting its stability'. According to the charge, General Phao had ordered the arrest of the director for alleged Communism, but Phao also 'intended to replace him as chief shareholder of the *Phim Thai* and *Siam Nikorn*'. The director, however, refused to sell his shares and refused to talk about Communists. So 'policemen and others were hired to get rid of Nai Aree'.

Another ex-deputy, whose 'disappearance' had long stirred speculation, was definitely dead, said a witness, a driver to a Police Colonel, in November 1958. A further witness told the court he had driven the deputy, late in 1954, just beyond Bangkok; he heard sounds in the back seat and saw him struggling with his captors. Later that evening the witness saw

* Reports of the trials: *Bangkok Post*, October 1, 1959; August 28 and September 26, 1958; January 25, 1958; and November 11, 1958.

two bodies trussed up and tied to cement posts. The bodies were driven away and put in a boat which was rowed out to the middle of the river. Next day he helped to dismantle an Austin car reported to have been driven by the victim on the day he 'disappeared'. At night, the scrap from the car was put into the launch and 'thrown bit by bit into the river as the launch progressed until there was no more iron left'.

As for Phao's 'Knights', those most involved in his crimes fled with their chief. The newspaper *Siam Nikorn* reported in 1958 that two of his Police Colonels were preparing to leave Europe for South America, a third was engaged in industry in Malaya, a fourth had stayed in the United States, and another 'is now in Laos and is doing a roaring business in smuggling, especially of armaments'.

PRESENT UNCERTAINTIES

Thai politicians, now freed from police persecution, are still subject to martial law. An unfortunate effect of martial law is that it indiscriminately suppresses all forms of political activity, both good and bad. Yet martial law is so convenient, from the point of view of a strong administration, that it tends to be retained long after the immediate causes that promoted it. Taiwan, for example, has been under martial law ever since the Nationalists left the mainland; Indonesia since the revolt of 1957 and Pakistan* and Thailand since 1958.

The results of this are threefold. First, political activity is driven underground, to the benefit of those who are best prepared for conspiracies. Second, as there is no legal outlet for politics, normal social or cultural activities may come under suspicion as a cover for subversion. Finally, legitimate griev-ances which can be brought into the open under a free system often become distorted and exaggerated under control.

Suspicions thrive in an atmosphere of uncertainty. Thai students who wish to demonstrate for jobs or against higher fees are warned against being exploited 'by a third hand'. This sinister phrase is constantly invoked in troublesome situations; it usually refers to Communists, though it may denote any

* Martial law ended in June 1962 when the new Constitution came into effect.

outside group, or even have no specific bearing at all, being but a vague incantation of customary effect. In this atmosphere, monkish protests over appointments to the hierarchy are seen as Communist intrigues, while forging lottery tickets and smuggling become deliberate attempts to subvert the Thai economy.

High officials of the Ministry of the Interior reported in July 1960 that Communist agents were, firstly, using lowly-educated persons as tools to spread rumours, secondly, spreading rumours about disputes among high government and military officials, and thirdly, alleging in coffee-shops and other public places the 'instability' of the Government. Rumours, disputes and allegations are the stuff of political life under martial law.

Attribution to the Communists, however, only flatters the Party*—a mysterious body of no great influence among the Thais (as distinct from local Chinese)—and undervalues the significance of other political forces, each associated with a dominant personality: Pibun, Pridi, Khuang and Thep Chotinuchit, the socialist leader from the North-East.

PIBUN

Nai Plaek Kheetasangha—as he was then—graduated from the army cadet college in Bangkok and pursued military studies in France. He was a major at the time of the 1932 coup which ended absolute monarchy. A year later he defeated a royalist rebellion. In 1934 (at the age of thirty-seven) he was Minister of Defence, Colonel and Deputy Commander-in-Chief. After four years he was Prime Minister. 'He is unusually handsome,' Professor K. P. Landon wrote at that time, 'with a crest of thick black hair and bold clear eyes. He is agile physically and quick in his thinking, a man of action.'

With the rise of Pibun—Field Marshal P. Pibun Songgram

* One of its rare pronouncements was made by the Thai delegate to the North Korean Communist Party Congress of September 1961. 'The Communist Party of Thailand,' said the un-named delegate, 'calls for the establishment of a patriotic, democratic united front for driving out us imperialism from Thailand, overthrowing the teacherous, dictatorial Sarit government, and for independence, neutrality, peace and democracy. It will put up an unyielding struggle by relying upon the popular masses and organizing and mobilizing them.'

is his 'position' name—went the rise of the military. Landon points out that in the first four years after the coup the military budget almost doubled. The actual rate of increase in the education budget was even greater, but the total amount came to less than half that for defence. This military emphasis met considerable opposition from the elected representatives in the Assembly, who desired heavier expenditure on roads, education and economic improvement. Landon observes (in *Siam in Transition*):

'The military emphasis seems out of character. The national character is peaceful and quiet. Many Thai admit frankly that they are too soft-hearted for war, for the destruction of human life. To many it seems a step backward. However, new times have come to Thailand. The country has been placarded with the picture of a soldier shaking his fist in the air. It bears the announcement that the kingdom is home, and the military is the fence about the home.'

Eleven of the twenty-one members of the State Council in 1938 were military; fifty-three of the seventy-eight nominated deputies ('second category') in 1937 were also military—but only eight of the seventy-eight elected deputies. The Premier from 1933–38, Phya Bahon, was also Commander-in-Chief. The change from rule by the royal family to rule by a strong military minority has been radical, Landon reports. Yet the people have remained quiet under the change.

Only the moderating influence of Bahon could have kept the balance between the liberals and the militarists, Sir Josiah Crosby, then British Minister to Bangkok, has observed. With the resignation of Bahon, constitutional experiment had failed. Pibun became 'Leader' and expressed open admiration for dictatorship: 'it is characteristic of the Siamese,' says Crosby, 'that they like to be in the fashion.' Ugly office blocks were put up along Rajadamnoen Avenue in emulation of the Axis Powers. 'Thailand' was to be the land of all the Thais, claiming Shans, Laos and even the Thais of South-West China for the fatherland.

Overthrown in 1944 by the pressure of Pridi and the Free Thais and of Allied successes against the Japanese, Pibun staged a successful coup in 1947. For nearly ten years he was in power, but with certain qualifications. As head of the administration he relinquished real control over the Army to Sarit. Secondly, he relied on his personal assistant, Colonel (later General) Phao, who was able to build up his own police empire—with the results that have been seen. Pibun, growing older and milder, could maintain his position only by maintaining a precarious balance between the two rivals, Phao and Sarit.

Seeking a broader basis of support, Pibun was genuinely impressed by the prestige and influence of the democratic leaders in Britain and America. Returning to Bangkok in 1955, he planned to restore 'democracy' to Thailand. As a sign of the times, Police General Phao wished all in 1956 'a happy and democratic New Year'. He went on to challenge the Democratic Party Leader, Khuang, to a cockfight on the Pramane Ground (the new 'Hyde Park') to see who was 'more democratic'.*

'Public opinion,' Pibun ventured a few days later, 'is to be the most powerful influence of the nation. People must keep a check on Government work' and help the 'drive against corruption'. But there need be no Cabinet reorganization, Pibun explained, because 'no Cabinet Minister has done anything really wrong'. In February the slogan was: 'The Government is going the whole way towards full democracy and there have been and will be no setbacks.' Whatever the criticisms, Pibun added in March, the Government should let a free press operate to 'prevent dictatorship taking over from democracy'.

The King's speech to the Assembly on National Day spoke of strictly upholding the Constitution, of better primary education, more democracy—replacement of nominated deputies—and gradual decentralization of authority down to village council level. Pibun set forth the virtues of democracy and the parliamentary system of government: people with the same political and economic beliefs, he said in Burkeian tones, gather together to form parties, to seek election to parliament and to set up a government if their candidates are elected to a majority of seats.

* Khuang retorted: 'Let Phao have a cockfight with someone born in the year of the Cock' (i.e. Pibun).

This was all very well till it was actually put to the test. The first election under the new system was to fill a seat at Uttaradit, North Thailand. With General Phao campaigning (not as Police Chief, of course, but as secretary-general of his political party) and with Pibun's timely allocation of five million baht (for roads, schools, irrigation and other development in the province), the ruling party won by a 'large margin'. Pibun added a rider on election procedure. It was 'within the rights' of the village head to suggest to residents whom they should vote for. As for soldiers, they were under discipline and it was 'more orderly' for them to poll in groups. Finally, 'Government and the governing party are hard to separate'.

During the general election campaign early in 1957 Pibun promised 'true' democracy 'from now on'. 'In the past I came into power through *coups d'état*. From now on I shall not seek power through *coups d'état*. I shall seek election.' The Finance Minister was then introduced (to tobacco workers) as a 'financial expert who is especially expert at increasing wages for labourers'. But promises were not enough. The Government relied on its trusted 'paratroopers' and 'fire cards' to win the February election. Popular revulsion was immediate. Two thousand Chulalongkorn University students brought the Thai flag to half-mast 'in memory of dead democracy'. They demanded a new election with students in the inspection committees and investigation of those who did wrong. A State of Emergency was proclaimed and Sarit—who openly sympathized with the students—took command. The situation improved and Phao found it no longer necessary to resign. Five uneasy months passed. In August, Sarit and his two Army deputies resigned from the Cabinet; sixty-two nominated deputies followed in September; the military group demanded the resignation of the Government and the dismissal of Phao. ('Beware of a third party trying to intervene in the present crisis,' cried an Air Marshal loyal to Pibun.) On September 16, 1957, Sarit seized power and Phao and Pibun fled.

A year later, in Tokyo, Marshal Pibun philosophically observed: 'If in four years or five years my party comes up again and public opinion supports it, then I must say that I am not playing with politics but politics can play with me. That depends on the future situation and none of us knows that. . . .'

PRIDI

Pridi Panomyong (also known by his title-name Luang Pradist Manudharm) comes of a well-to-do provincial family. Like Pibun, he studied in France. Before 1932 he was Professor of Law at Chulalongkorn University and Secretary of the Bar Association. 'At the time of the revolution,' Landon writes, 'Luang Pradist was about thirty years old. In appearance he is a typical Thai, slim, strong, with heavy black hair cropped close in the German style. His face is unremarkable except for his very healthy looking skin and unusually brilliant eyes, which are partly veiled under heavy lids. He is direct and friendly in his personality and has a manner that wins men. He is tremendously active mentally and physically and the author of numerous books. His mind is extraordinarily brilliant.'

As the civilian inspirer of the revolution against absolute monarchy, Pridi proposed radical economic reform for the country. His Plan, presented in 1933, was for the Government to buy up all farming land, issuing bonds according to its value. The farmers would become Government employees: they would work for the Government and in return receive salary and pension. The Government would take over the main business of the nation—the production and sale of rice—thus eliminating the middleman and wholesalers who were usually Chinese. Not much money would be needed, Pridi explained, because the workers would be required to buy from Government stores.

Surprisingly, a majority of a high-level committee favoured a trial. But the conservative and royalist Premier (Phya Manopakorn) opposed it. Instead, he suggested a co-operative, rather than collective, society. More credit should be granted to the peasants and credit stores should be set up where they could buy supplies at cost. Granaries should be established locally to buy and ship paddy to Bangkok, and co-operative rice mills would export it abroad. Settlement schemes should be drawn up for those without land.

The Premier announced that the State Council could not agree on Pridi's Plan. His own supporters considered it 'communistic'. There were bitter arguments in the Assembly. Parliament was prorogued and the Ministry of the Interior forbade any public discussion: no details of the Plan were ever published in Thailand. Pridi resigned from the Council and sailed for Europe. Meanwhile, an 'Act concerning Communism' was passed, specially condemning nationalization of land, industry, capital and labour. Only when the Manopakorn Cabinet was overthrown, and the revolutionaries returned to power, did Pridi come back to Thailand. A special Commission of Investigation cleared Pridi, in 1934, of the charge of Communism—but the Plan was never revived. Pridi, who was appointed Minister of the Interior, Foreign Minister and finally Finance Minister in 1938, carried out orthodox, nationalistic policies.

All the same, the Plan is a remarkable document. (The complete text is given in Landon's *Siam in Transition*.) It is clearly inspired by both the French and Russian Revolutions— French, in that it suggests an ideal society, sought through the use of reason; Russian in its antipathy to 'private enterprise' and its belief in State control; and purely Thai in its opening paragraphs:

'Sympathy springs up unbidden,' Pridi declares, 'at the sight of their (the poor) inadequate food, clothing and shelter, the bare necessities which are all they have in life. Even when they have food for today, tomorrow and the days after tomorrow are unpredictable. The future is at best precarious. When one considers the uncertainties of life, the way in which we are all subject to old age and disease, one may well ask whether those who, while they are still well and strong are so poor and needy, will in such eventualities have even food to eat.'

People in the middle and wealthy classes are subject to the same uncertainties. 'The inheritance left a son melts away and is gone, and the once rich heir becomes poor. Such examples show the impermanence of wealth.' Scholars, Pridi says, consider that the only solution is for the Government to ensure the wellbeing of its citizens: 'when the Government can give such guarantees, every citizen will sleep in peace.'

The Plan is to issue monthly wages to all people. 'It is well known that all Thais want to work for the Government and that they like to receive regular salary.' Where is the money to come from? But money is only something to be exchanged. The distribution of money is equivalent to the distribution of food, clothing and shelter. Government co-operative societies will in fact exchange material things for the wages the Government will pay the people.

The present system is inefficient. 'As a direct result of the system of private enterprise much manpower is wasted, labour efficiency is lowered, there is a lack of tools and machinery needed to increase production, and there are social parasites whose labour value is negative.' The peasants till their fields, on average, only six months in the year. Thus six months of their time is wasted. Private enterprise cannot do anything. The only way is 'for the Government to draw up a national economic plan'.

When each works for himself, labour is also wasted: it is better to co-operate. For example, 'household work, such as the preparation of food, could be lessened by a club system. A shop could be established to provide the day's food for all the people in a community' (a prophecy indeed). Machinery, too, multiplies the efficiency of labour. Thai people are slight in body, not as strong as Chinese and foreigners. So 'if we depend upon manpower in our various enterprises we can never compete'.

'Social parasites' waste labour. 'There is no better method than government control of the economic system, because the Government can require all people to work and can make social parasites become producers for the good of the nation.' But there must be co-operation between rich and poor, and use of legal methods. 'The Government must not destroy the wealthy class.'

Land-ownership, he affirms, has proved a liability rather than an asset: 99 per cent of the farmers are in debt. In fact, if the Government offered to buy land at a fair price, farmers, owners and creditors 'would be delighted'.

'It is the nature of the Thai people to like to work for the Government', so 'there will be no difficulty in enlisting the entire nation as Government employees'. After fifty-five, a pension; before eighteen, school and light work, and salaries payable according to education, strength and abilities, though those engaged in private professions may opt out of the Plan. After holidays have been deducted, 'the people as a whole will be provided with work for the entire year'.

'It is true that there will be less freedom of a sort,' Pridi admits, 'but the loss in personal liberty will be more than com-

F

pensated for by the general increase in the happiness and prosperity of the people as a whole.' The Plan is a system 'by which we can press forward to this golden age. . . .'

Delightfully though it is put—and this is typical of the Thai people—the implications are alarming—in Chinese hands we can clearly see how alarming. Moreover, for all its reasoning, it is based on three assumptions, that land is unprofitable, that all Thais wish to be officials, and that they are ready to work all the year.

Even at that time, the era of world-wide depressions, it is doubtful if the peasants were '99 per cent' in debt. Nowadays the figure is not more than 20 per cent. What in fact is remarkable is Thai persistence in growing rice; it is only in towns that the people wish to become officials. Pridi's Plan is a sort of Communism without compulsion—but it would take considerable compulsion to get Thai people (even 'officials') to work every day.

Nor should the authoritarian strain be ignored. Pridi led the 'civilian', as opposed to the military group, but was 'democratic' only in contrast with Pibun. When his turn came, after the war, his first three Premiers (Khuang and Seni, of the later Democratic Party, and Tawee Bunyaket, now the investment chief) were short-lived. Pridi's regime was dogged by ill fate. Besides the problems of corruption and inflation, stemming from the war years, he became responsible for rice 'reparations' to Japanese-occupied countries and for the surrender of the Cambodian and other areas seized by Pibun.

Then came the death of the young king. This strange tragedy has never been satisfactorily explained. Pridi's investigation commission posed three questions. Was it suicide, murder or accident? Pibun's commission, set up after his seizure of power a year later, clearly implicated Pridi. Yet for Pridi there was nothing to gain by murder, and everything—in view of the profound respect among the people for monarchy—to lose. It is inconceivable that Pridi would have signed his own death warrant by such a deed, but it is possible that some fanatic did it, unauthorized, for Pridi's gain. Whatever the truth—and it is said that members of the royal family alone know it—the matter proved politically fatal to Pridi.

Pridi fled in November 1947. Two foreigners helped him to

escape into the Gulf of Thailand by motor boat. A storm arose, but he was picked up by a tanker and taken to Singapore. From fear of extradition he dared not stay in Singapore longer. He went in succession to Saigon, Hong Kong and finally Shanghai, which was still in Nationalist hands. A few days later the Communists took over. Pridi moved to Peking and, in 1956, settled in Canton.

Had Pridi remained in South-East Asia, or fled to India, the history of Thailand might have been very different, but the flight to China was irrevocable; in fact he had no option. 'The November (1947) Coup Group staged its *coup* in order to rid Thailand of former Premier Pridi Panomyong,' said General Prapart in December 1956 (he was then Deputy Commander of the 1st Army and is now Minister of the Interior). 'Believing that he is a Communist, the Group is unwilling to have Nai Pridi return here without having to go to court for trial in the King's Death Case.'

Pridi was not a Communist when he fled; nor is there evidence that he has become one. His public statements in exile have been more in support of his own position in Thailand than of either Chinese or local Communist policies. But there is no doubt that he relies on the Chinese for an eventual return and that the Chinese are prepared to back him.

General Phao, talking to newsmen in July 1956, affirmed that Pridi was living with his family in China 'in the position of a guest, without engaging in political activities'. The following April, Pridi's wife returned to Thailand to visit her mother. She was met at Bangkok by numerous relatives and friends; among them was her son, who had been released on bail in the November 1952 'Communist conspiracy' case. Pridi, she said, was studying agriculture in Kwangtung Province. He was not required to do work, and his health and living expenses were paid by the Chinese Government. She denied that he had been gathering troops for an attack on Thailand (suggested by a Thai socialist leader) or had ever been in the Thai autonomous region, set up by China near the Thai and Lao frontiers. Pridi had, however, broadcast from Peking in 1954 in favour of the 'Thai Autonomous People's Government'.

During the curious evolution of Thai foreign policy under Pibun in 1956 and 1957 (which will be discussed later) devious approaches to China were made in an attempt at 'disengagement'. Left-wing visitors to China and the Chinese exiles played their part. A Moslem supporter of Pridi—who revealed the details of Pridi's escape—returned to Thailand early in 1956. He openly called for a *rapprochement* between Pridi and Pibun and even, for a time, joined the latter's Seri Manang-kasila Party.

A former deputy-chief of the Police Political Affairs Division under Pridi also returned from China in 1956. In January 1957 he formed a new political party (Sri-ariya-metrai, or Buddhist utopia party) which opposed, variously, war, military pacts (such as SEATO), 'aristocracy' and 'imperialism'. His party also urged the return of Pridi. By way of an interlude, the then Premier of Laos, Prince Souvanna Phouma, had met Pridi when on his tour of China in 1956. The Prince had been a fellow-student with Pridi in France. He spoke of Pridi's expressed desire to visit Laos and added that he, the Prince, would welcome him any time.

Newspaper interviews have also put Pridi's views before the Thai public—at least up to Sarit's resumption of power. In the Chinese Communist *Ta Kung Pao* (May 1957) Pridi declared that the United States was the obstacle preventing normal diplomatic relations between Thailand and China. The extreme left-wing Thai *Khao Pharb* early in October 1958, however, reported Pridi's approval of General Thanom's interim government. This was chiefly for 'making it possible for people to travel to China without meeting obstacles or being threatened with arrest'. The best policy, Pridi said, was a 'neutral or independent policy which looks after the interests of the Thai nation and people'.

'No one can say,' pointed out the independent *Siam Rath* in April 1959, 'that the politicians who supported Nai Pridi have ceased their underground activities in support of him. . . .'

KHUANG AND THE ANCIENT REGIME

Last of the 'three Luangs' (the others are Luang Pibun and Luang Pradist, i.e. Pridi) is Luang Kovit Aphaiwong. All three studied in France before the 1932 *coup* and took up positions in the constitutional government. All three have renounced the title of Luang—Luang Kovit is known as Nai Khuang. A close friend of Pridi, he accepted Pibun's pro-Japanese policy, became Premier under the auspices first of Pridi and later Pibun. Four times Premier, Khuang has never held office more than a few months each time.*

Khuang is the leader of the Democratic Party, which briefly flourished after the war and again during Pibun's democratic phase. Liberalism, Khuang says, is best for Thailand's economy: a liberal trading policy with free competition. Monopoly is undesirable because it enriches only a few, while official corruption must be uprooted. Khuang insisted during the 1956–57 election campaign that he would end the 'mystery' of the shooting of the four ex-Cabinet Ministers—'one of the most pressing questions in the public mind'—and, if elected Premier, that he would resist any further attempt to get rid of him by force.

Like the Pibun Government, he would not recognize Peking; Thailand should wait till China was admitted to the United Nations. Yet he alleged that General Phao had secretly sent 'visitors' to Pridi to seek Chinese aid and recognition. Pridi's part in these manoeuvres, he believed, was to use Pibun and Phao as instruments in his own attempt to regain power.

When told that the leader of the socialist 'Hyde Park Movement' had joined Pibun's party—'differences of opinion,' Pibun said, 'are an important part of democracy'—and asked why he should not also join, he retorted that he was no *muay lom*—a boxer bribed to lose his fight. Khuang's independence was justified not at the 'fixed' elections of February but at the free vote in December 1957. Thirty-nine Democrats were chosen in all, out of an elected house of 160; all but one of the Bangkok deputies were Democrats. The Democrats went on to win fourteen out of twenty-six seats in the by-elections held a few months later. For a year the Party maintained its critical stand, but was then suppressed with all other political groups on the

---

* An interesting account of pre-war and immediate post-war events is given in John Coast's *Some Aspects of Siamese Politics*, published in 1953, and in the sincere and moving story of Alexander MacDonald, founder of the 'Bangkok Post', *Bangkok Editor*, published in 1949.

outbreak of the Revolution. Yet Khuang, frivolous, irrepressible, forthright, shrewd and honest, conservative and royalist, represents, above all, the decencies of the past.

The great days of absolute monarchy, paradoxically, were the days of foreign advisers and experts. King Mongkut (1851–68) and King Chulalongkorn (1868–1910) had the wisdom to recognize the need for reform and the dexterity to use foreign help successfully, that is, to adopt the instrument of improvement without the colonial regime that went with it.

'At the head of the corps of advisers,' states Sir Josiah Crosby in *Siam at the Crossroads*, 'stood the General Adviser (also Adviser in Foreign Affairs) who was always American.' There was a succession of Financial and Judicial Advisers, all of them British, and British advisers to Customs, a British Director of Inland Revenue and a British head of the Bangkok Police. Most of the foreign instructors at the Ministry of Education were British, and there were British experts in Survey and Irrigation.

Danish officers were attached to the gendarmerie, and at one time served in the Navy. 'The post of Legislative Adviser was always held by a Frenchman, and there was a Legislative Commission composed of French experts, whose duty it was to draw up a series of Legal Codes.' Bangkok City Engineers were usually French. Italians were employed, however, in Public Works. Germans were attached to the Northern Railways, Britons and some Italians to the South. Germans for a time ran Posts and Telegraph. The Thais, Crosby reports, were eclectic in their choice, but the British predominated.

'Advisers to the Government'—the General, Financial, Judicial and Legislative Advisers—were consulted both on matters of policy and routine. The task of foreign diplomats, of which Sir Josiah was one, was chiefly to secure as large a share as possible of Government contracts for the Army, Navy, railways and irrigation, and 'to bring about the engagement of as many advisers of their own nationality as they could'.

The royal dynasty itself possessed remarkable talent. The first Chakri king was soldier, statesman and poet, the second poet and patron of the dance. King Mongkut (Rama IV), a monk for twenty-seven years before ascending the throne, studied English under American missionaries and Latin, mathe-

matics and astronomy from Bishop Pallegoix (the king died of a
fever caught while observing a solar eclipse). His son, King
Chulalongkorn, was ably assisted in his great task of reform
and modernization by his brothers and half-brothers. Among
them were Prince Devawong, over forty years Minister of
Foreign Affairs; Prince Damrong, historian and archaeologist,
Minister of Education and of the Interior; Prince Narit,
designer of the Marble Temple; and Prince Vajirayana, the
Supreme Patriarch. King Vajiravud, the sixth king, poet,
playwright and patriot (though no statesman), was also
surrounded by Princes, some of high ability. It was the ability of
some and the incompetence of others which prevented any
concession being made to the rising soldiers and civilians, and
thus precipitated in the next reign the downfall of absolute
monarchy.

Such is benevolent despotism. But there is another side, noted
by the French naturalist and explorer, Henri Mouhot. Writing
during the reign of King Mongkut (*Voyage dans les Royaumes de
Siam, de Cambodge, de Laos*, published after his death in Laos, in
1868), Mouhot reports: 'Officials are poorly paid, badly controlled and never surveyed; the result is easy to discover, they
all misappropriate funds; the king knows it and closes his eyes,
either because of the great number who would have to be
punished, or else because such matters are not worth taking up
a moment of his time. The provinces are milch cows for their
governors, who make them yield whatever they can give. . . .
Should the higher officials wish to build a house, the labour
costs them nothing; they requisition the people and rattan
staves assure their activity. . . .'

Bishop Pallegoix supports this account. 'In general,' he
writes, 'the Siamese have a horror of theft, which does not
mean there are no thieves among them; for the princes and
mandarins apply themselves continually to extorting money
from their subordinates; the big chiefs steal from lesser chiefs
and those steal from the poor.' (The 'first Hell', in Thai
popular Buddhism, is reserved for 'those who have killed
animals, thieves, rapists, kings who have carried out unjust
wars, and the oppressors of the poor. . . .')

It is true that forced labour, the *corvée*, was abolished before
the end of the last century, and slavery early in the twentieth,

but enlightenment at the centre does not always penetrate into the interior.

SOCIALISM AND THE NORTH-EAST

If Pridi is the father of socialism in Thailand his disciple is a provincial, and the source of his strength lies in the poorest and most neglected of the provinces—those of the North-East. Thep Chotinuchit, son of a lawyer-official, has had an unusually varied career. Gaining degrees in law and economics at Bangkok, his first job was managing a Government opium den. In 1937 he was appointed judge, and ten years later was elected deputy from Sisaket, in the North-East. From 1949–51 he was deputy-Minister of Commerce in the Pibun Government.*

Thep denies Marxism or even Pridi's 'state socialism', Wilson asserts. He supports full parliamentary government and local self-government. But the 'State shall promote, advise, initiate and assist or control production, including transportation and distribution'. This may be 'socialism', though the Vice-Chairman of the Asian Socialist Conference, passing through Bangkok in January 1957, was not sure that Thep really was a socialist. Thep himself was unable to attend the conference at Rangoon as his passport had been seized following a visit to China.

Thep's critics call him a Communist, his friends a socialist and neutrals an opportunist. His attitudes are varied: he has openly expressed support for popular independence in Hungary and Poland while he has equally condemned American policy and SEATO. After the overthrow of Pibun, he urged 'continued promotion of religion and the support of monarchy, as well as co-operation with capitalists, at least at this stage'.

Thep moved close to a policy during the post-Pibun election campaign. His 'Socialist Front' made five pledges: first, to develop the economy with proper planning—'it calls for a planned economy,' he said later, 'beneficial to the producer and the middleman and the consumer. We cannot simply cut off the middlemen, who after all are also Thai citizens who have a

* David A. Wilson, 'Thailand and Marxism', in *Marxism and South East Asia*, edited by F. N. Trager.

place in the national economy'. Secondly, to ensure justice to capitalists, people with ability and the labourers—'We still have need of capitalists; we shall get rid of them later.' Thirdly, to use most of the budget for the happiness of the people. Fourthly, to abrogate all laws against the rights of the people, i.e. the Anti-Communist Act. And finally, to repeal all unjust taxes.

As for foreign policy, it would be 'neutral and independent', accepting only unconditional aid. 'My party is not anti-American: it is not anti any nation; it would accept American aid or aid from any other country if the aid is really given without strings.' There should be 'free trade' with all countries —including China. The world should be rid of military pacts like SEATO. Finally Thep believed in the party astrologer's forecast that the nation would go left. (The astrologer himself was a candidate and forecast his own victory.)

Though vague and unalarming on the home front, Thep campaigned vigorously against the country's pro-Western foreign policy, and notably its commitment to SEATO. In this he undoubtedly followed the Communist line. In reality he had little choice. Not differing very explicitly from the Government's domestic policy—as Khuang did—Thep had to oppose something.

Thep's strength was the poverty and discontent of the North-East. The drought that season was the worst in forty years. 'There has been little or no rain,' the Government said. 'Farmers are suffering. There is no water to feed the plants. In some places there are only few seeds, and these have been planted. Lack of water is causing the death of these young plants and there are no seeds to be sown.' As a reporter noted of one socialist candidate, accused by his rivals of being a Communist and receiving Communist funds: 'the people (of the North-East) do not understand about Communism, being only aware of the hard facts of their life.'

Curiously, Thep's own 'Economist' party won more seats (eight) under Pibun's elections than at the free elections at the end of 1957 (only six). But they were all in the North-East. For a year Thep led the parliamentary assault against the West; then he and his followers were arrested under martial law. They were removed to gaol, where they still lie.

COMMUNISM

Individual Communists there are in Thailand, as well as various shades of 'leftist' opinion (often taken for Communism), but the activities of the Thai Communist Party are subdued and mysterious. For one thing it is illegal, and has been for most of its existence. In 1946, briefly legalized in return for Soviet acceptance of Thailand in the United Nations, its Secretary-General was Prasad Sabsunthorn, a former university lecturer and deputy. A very moderate programme was adopted, states J. H. Brimmell (in *Communism in South-East Asia: a political analysis*): co-operation with all who favoured an independent democratic Thailand; recognition of democratic freedoms, minority rights, political parties; improved living standards for workers, social insurance, promotion of agriculture, rent reduction and so on.

The Party's second national conference, Brimmell reports, was early in 1952, under a new Secretary-General, Prasong Vongvivat. (His predecessor slipped over to Peking for a peace rally, and stayed there.) The conference set up a 'Thai National Liberation Organization' though, as Brimmell observes, there was no national liberation movement to lead; nor was there peasant unrest as in the Philippines nor any general malaise as in Burma.

Later that year the blow fell. General Phao discovered a plot to foment a Communist revolution, force the king to abdicate, carry out sabotage, murder officials and seize strongpoints. Many political opponents of the regime were arrested and no doubt some Communists. From 1932–50, 991 persons were arrested under the anti-Communist acts, the HRAF handbook on Thailand states, but only sixteen were convicted.

The Chinese in particular suffered from this repression. Skinner (in *Chinese Society in Thailand*) cites an estimate, by Phao, of 2,000 Thai and 10,000 Chinese Communists. More arrests followed in 1953 and 1954. It was not till Bandung and Pibun's 'conversion' to democracy that the Chinese became 'friendly aliens' once more. Meanwhile the 'Un-Thai Activities Act' was held in reserve. This broad weapon provided for five to ten years' imprisonment for those, quoted by Skinner, who 'incite, advise, coerce others to act as Communists or propagate

Communism, associate or rally, or are accomplices of Communism, or prepare to do something Communistic. . . .'

Pibun still 'campaigned against the Reds'. Reading a newspaper headline, 'Reds Fix Date for Invasion of Thailand in December (1956)', the Prime Minister wrote, 'Send this to the Police Department to consider, investigate and suppress.' Shortly afterwards, however, he declared that 'Communist activities have declined. . . . Even Russia may be turning from Communism to democracy.'

Pibun did observe that labour was infiltrated. So also were Thai students. Seni Pramoj, a distinguished lawyer and former Premier, in November 1957 accused the 'Student Committee' of Thammasat University of publishing an 'ideology hostile to Thai traditions'. 'Yes, there is political interference in the university,' its Secretary-General admitted. 'But I cannot do anything. I am only in charge of administration.' A Police General reported that Thai and *Lukchin* (Thai-born Chinese) youths abroad were forming a bridgehead for Communist infiltration. The Thai students came mainly from England and other countries where he said they were attracted to Marxism; the *Lukchin* chiefly from Peking University: both types 'have good minds and come from reasonably respected families'.

At this time, shortly after the coup against Pibun, the Military Group accused the Chinese Communists of opening a ten million baht bank credit in Hong Kong to finance press propaganda in Thailand. They were shipping newsprint and printing presses to left-wing Thai and Chinese newspapers in Bangkok. The latter, in return, attacked SEATO, encouraged neutralism and offered trade prospects with China. Two newspapers, during the interregnum between Pibun and Sarit, did become notorious for their views: one was subsidized by the Russians, the other by the Chinese.

Government, after three months under Pote Sarasin* (preparing for elections), was in the hands of General Thanom Kittikachorn, Sarit's deputy. Thanom, a friendly but unreliable figure, found it difficult to cope with the outstanding economic

---

* Pote Sarasin, trained as a lawyer, a wealthy businessman and man of independent character, was formerly Foreign Minister and Ambassador in Washington and is at present Secretary-General of SEATO.

and political problems. But the public welcomed the removal of police power, and the left wing, stirring under Pibun, revived. Even the Government went in for a policy of 'mild socialism'. The Unionist Party, its main supporters in parliament, contained 'leftists, socialists, rightists, conservatives, middle of the roaders, Hyde Parkers, and cast-offs from other parties'.

The Government was divided against itself, discontent grew and 'leftist' activities increased. By Western standards they were not very sinister. A group of journalists visited Russia, a cultural delegation China. Fifteen deputies, including four Socialists, two Democrats and one from the Government party —now the 'National Socialists'—visited both countries. The delegation was led by a Democratic Admiral, recently released from gaol after serving eight years for his part in the Navy revolt. 'Front' activities were the order of the day.

THE REVOLUTION
AND THE SOCIAL ORDER

Throughout 1958 there were rumours of plots and dissension. In June the Democrats and Independents proposed a general debate against the Government: 'There has been much corruption in Government circles,' they declared. 'The Government cannot protect the lives and property of the people as shown in the current contagious epidemic (cholera) and the rise in the crime rate.' Inefficiency in education 'causes problems for students and parents'. Above all, 'the Government has failed in its economic and financial policies, causing a high cost of living, and has shown that it cannot raise the living standard of the people'. Anxious deputies recalled that following every previous 'general debate' there had been a *coup*, from 1947 (by Pibun) to 1957 (against Pibun). However, Marshal Sarit flew in, averted the debate and postponed the *coup*.

Seven years before, the Army Commander-in-Chief had overthrown the Government, dissolved the National Assembly and appointed a provisional Executive Council (three from each of the armed services). The reason for this was that the Government had failed to suppress corruption or to solve the problem of Communism. Marshal Pibun remained Premier, but the 1947 Constitution was abolished and the previous one of 1932 restored.

In October 1958, Marshal Sarit returned a second time from England, where he was convalescing after a serious operation, overthrew the Government of his own deputy (General Thanom), abrogated the Constitution, dissolved the Assembly and abolished existing political parties. The Marshal formed a Revolutionary Party headed by himself, as Supreme Commander of the Armed Forces, to control the administration. Martial law was enforced, since corruption was increasing, the economic situation was precarious and Communist infiltration had become intensified.

The first announcement came over Radio Thailand at 9 p.m., October 20, 1958. It said that the Revolutionary Party comprising army, navy, air force, police officers and civilians had assumed control as from that hour. Later announcements stated that the Party had seized power in the name of the people 'because of internal pressures and pressures from abroad, and particularly because of the increasingly serious nature of the Communist threat to Thailand'. Newspapers causing disturbances would be severely dealt with. Under-secretaries and high officials should report to Party head-quarters at the Army Conference Hall. Peace and order should be maintained; merchants must not hoard goods or raise prices.

'Thailand,' the *Times of India's* Asian Notebook reported on November 16, '. . . is in the grip of an acute economic crisis. . . . Today Bangkok is seething with unrest. There is mounting unemployment; business is down; and foreign exchange reserves have diminished to the lowest in Thailand's history. Agitation in these circumstances is natural, but it is suppressed with an iron hand. . . .' This was written nearly a month after the event; in fact, only a day after, it was remarkable to note the almost total absence of anything unusual in Bangkok beyond a few trenches, sandbags and soldiers at various cross-roads and certain streets barred to traffic. The only visible sign of unrest was on the faces of former deputies who turned up at the Assembly to collect their last wages.

Only on the Left was there confusion and dismay. From 2 a.m. until dawn police searched the offices of three Thai and two Chinese newspapers, arresting thirty-six editors and reporters. Visitors to China or Russia and traders in Chinese goods were also held. Police took into custody five former exiles from China (followers of Pridi), two students and four labour leaders. On the 22nd, twelve newspapers were closed and Thep, chairman of the Socialist Front, was arrested. Police later arrested forty-seven persons in Sisaket Province on charges of 'engaging in Communist activities'. Seized documents, they said, 'clearly showed that Nai Thep Chotinuchit was director of Communist activities in the North-East'.

Sixteen Chinese were in the first batch of arrests; among them were two officials of the leading Chinese charity organization, the President of the Postal Remittance Association (to China), several journalists, a teacher and a doctor. Hundreds of reels of film from Communist countries and Russian and Chinese books and pamphlets were impounded. Chinese schools in Bangkok and up-country were searched. Vietnamese Communists brought by rail from the North-East were also arrested. Over two hundred suspects were put in gaol.

The most dramatic action occurred eight months later, at the end of June 1959. Four police patrols approached a small house in a *durian* (tropical fruit) plantation in Thonburi. They were hampered by a moat, a fierce dog and an electric warning system. Two men were caught escaping and a third was found hiding in a hole in the ground. He was unshaven, explaining to the police he wished to look like Ho Chi Minh. Searching the area, the police found field telephones, type-writers, a telegraph transmitter, a duplicator, stencils, leaflets, radio receiving sets, medals from Communist countries, four guns, a copy of Plato's *Republic* with pages hollowed out to hold a pistol, a wooden 'peace dove' and photographs of Mao Tse-tung.

Suppachai, the arrested man, confessed to having issued Communist statements and to have printed 'protests' from *samlor* (pedicab) drivers. The police later reported that Suppachai was 'a person of good standing', a wartime student in Japan, who became secretary-general of the Thai Central Labour Union and as such received orders and instructions from the Communist World Federation of Trade Unions. Shortly after, he was executed.

'Evils and corrupt practices had multiplied'; thus Sarit

explained (in December 1958) the reason for the drastic action
taken by the Revolutionary Party. 'Subversion of the Government was the order of the day, taking advantage of loopholes in
the Constitution and of defects and shortcomings in the
administrative procedures. Communist infiltration and subversion had intensified; no institution was immune from the
contamination. The National Assembly, the press and certain
labour circles had also succumbed. . . .'

Parliament
The fallen deputies were presumably members of the Socialist
Front, as well as certain Independents and Democrats. In
general, the Assembly was more ineffective than seditious (see
above).

Press
The press was certainly more affected. Communist or Left-
wing journalists—they are difficult to distinguish since both
support neutralism in opposition to the prevailing foreign
policy—played a considerable role. They were generally more
active and intelligent than their orthodox colleagues, and they
believed in a cause and were prepared to work for it. Journalism
in Thailand is poorly paid and ill-regarded, and able men,
unless they are dedicated, prefer to go elsewhere.

Too many small newspapers—usually personal mouthpieces
of aspiring politicians, policemen or soldiers—exist, with small
circulations. They rely on sex, crime and scurrility to increase
their sales. A notable exception is Kukrit's *Siam Rath*, critical,
balanced and influential; *Siam Nikorn* is another. The former
has one of the largest circulations, about 20,000 a day. Total
circulation of newspapers is not much more than 200,000 a day,
mostly in Bangkok, and all are typeset by hand, as the cost of
Linotype machines is prohibitive. Nor can the average wage-
earner afford to spend up to 5 per cent of his daily income
(50 satang to one baht) on a newspaper, except when the
lottery results are announced.

The ill-effects of irresponsible reporting are easily recogniz-
able. Marshal Sarit urged newspapers not to publish alarming
reports under such headlines as 'Chinese Reds Approach Near
Thai Border'. As a result he had been asked: 'Where are we

going to be evacuated to?' The Prime Minister added: 'Such kind of reporting will create excitement, cause people to withdraw money from banks, cause prices to be raised.' False reports on his health were also going round; rumours had even spread, the Marshal complained, that he was ill and dying, or had been stabbed to death by a woman!

Trade Unions

Trade unions, also on the Marshal's list, are of course one of the main targets for Communist subversion. For one thing they are necessarily proletarian in character and for another they are a 'mass organization', the necessary counterpart to the bourgeois intellectuals who run the Party. In Thailand, the Central Labour Union quickly succumbed. Set up after the war, as the HRAF handbook relates, it included railway, tram and bus drivers, dockers, rice and sawmill workers. Its original leaders were Thai, mainly lawyers; its members, up to 70,000, mainly Chinese. In 1949 it affiliated with the World Federation of Trade Unions, a body which had been founded in the hope of achieving allied unity but which instead came under Communist control.

The Central Labour Union was banned, and its leaders went underground. Meanwhile Pibun had organized the Thai National Trade Union Congress, with a total membership of 75,000. It received an annual Government subsidy of 200,000 baht, and concerned itself, the handbook reports, with labour welfare and measures of labour-capital co-operation. Its directors, according to David A. Wilson, were Army and Police Officers; its members, agricultural workers, fishermen and *samlor* drivers. Phao, too, set up his own Free Workmen's Association of Thailand with (mostly Chinese) dock, rice, mill and factory workers.

During Pibun's democratic phase a draft labour bill was prepared (June 1956) to consider disputes, general working conditions, relations with employers and research on unemployment. Authority was given to organize trade unions, to protect their right to strike and to establish a forty-eight-hour working week. Pibun said it was his 'definite policy' to promote industry and spoke of establishing normal trade relations with Peking—both a sop to left-wing opinion. Sixteen unions were recognized in February 1957, including workers of Bangkok port, two bus companies, the Government Tobacco Monopoly, beer, shoes, construction, electricity and oil companies. Strikes had previously broken out at several of these companies for higher wages, but in May 1957 the Labour Relations Board opposed raising the minimum wage of railway workers from 17 to 20 baht—up to 7 shillings or one dollar—a day, saying that a rush of demands would break out if it did.

Thai trade unions have had an unhappy history. Directed either openly by the Government or secretly by pro-Communists, they have been unable to produce true leaders supporting labour interests and divorced from personal ambition. As with democracy, in which the unions should play a vital part, the ground was not prepared and self-government was not achieved.

Students

Student problems (briefly mentioned, in a subversive capacity, above) are quite different. Students are individuals, only formally part of a collective organization, soon to be dispersed. Labour leaders have a responsibility to their unions, students to themselves. Whatever influences they may be exposed to, experience of itself, in an open society, should modify the claims of doctrines. Repression, though it discourages the many from dabbling in 'dangerous thoughts', only hardens the convictions —because it confirms them—of the few who believe. And even for those who conform, the result is ignorance or prejudice, which are poor guides to behaviour. Students resort to criticism, even opposition, but not to subversion.

In satisfactory conditions, Communism normally appeals only to a small minority. Only 1 per cent of the Thai students who polled in 1958 (*Public Opinion among Thai Students*, University of Thammasat) believed that Communism offered the best prospects for their country; 75 per cent chose democracy and 21 per cent 'neutralism'. The survey covered 120 students from Thammasat, the University of Moral and Political Sciences, founded by Pridi, and 154 students from the Agriculture, Medical and Education Universities (strictly faculties) and the Technical Institute, but none from the senior University, Chulalongkorn. Their attitudes are of considerable interest.

G

Over half the students wished for a career as 'government officials' in the true Thai tradition. 'Education' topped all values; 'conservatism' and 'Westernization' alike were almost totally rejected. The nature of the Thai people, the students considered, was carefree, generous, gentle and religious (in this order of choice), but also lazy, selfish and hot-headed. They ought to be, on the other hand, more ambitious, self-confident, nationalistic and progressive. The person they were most likely to trust was the teacher, then the priest and doctor, while the least likely were the politician, the journalist and the business-man, in that order.

Eighty to ninety per cent thought the results of the 1932 *coup* (ending Absolute Monarchy) were 'mainly good', 60 to 75 per cent saw in it the 'beginning of democracy'. The worst features were 'corruption' (leading to further *coups*) according to 26 per cent, and 'no real democracy' according to 17 per cent. Twenty-eight per cent said there were *no* bad results. Thailand's greatest need was 'good education for all' (65 per cent), 'more industrialization' (35 per cent) and 'a higher standard of living' (32 per cent). Sixty per cent 'very much liked' and another 35 per cent 'liked' democracy, because it was 'fair and free'. Forty-one per cent liked, 13 per cent very much liked, neutralism; 80 per cent disliked it, 37 per cent had 'no feeling'.

Half the students had 'no feeling' about either nationalism, independence or socialism (all of which were 'liked' by a third). Capitalism was widely disliked (by over two-thirds), imperialism slightly less so. Communism was very much disliked by almost a third and disliked by nearly half (people under Communism had 'no freedom and no hope'); but a fifth had no feelings, while 4 per cent liked it. Dictatorship—the poll was carried out during the relaxed days of the Thanom Government—was even more firmly rejected. To summarize their reactions, a neutralist foreign policy would be popular, while democracy offered the best prospects.

NEW REGIME

Two things are needed by all states, efficient administration and security, and one thing by most states, and that is not so much democracy as a system, and the knowledge of how to make it work. In Thailand, good government as an aim has obviously been set before self-government and the economic ministries have not been impeded. But politics is a holding operation; it is a reversion to the practice, though not the form, of absolute monarchy. (In fact the king, as constitutional monarch, is more highly regarded then before.) There is one leader, whose word is law. No criticism is permitted, no form of opposition allowed, but able ministers are encouraged and foreign experts continue to be employed. Political progress is blocked, or rather, as the Government would see it, the destructive energies released under democracy are controlled or diverted to economic advantage.

The Government, formed in February 1959, is headed by Marshal Sarit and his two deputies, General Thanom (Minister of Defence) and General Prapart Charusathien (Minister of the Interior). General Thanom and Prince Wan, in his customary role of adviser to the Government, are Deputy Premiers. A number of important ministers were brought in from the administration or civil service. Thanat Khoman, Foreign Minister, was Ambassador in Washington. Boon Charoenchai, Minister of Industry and Sunthorn Hongladarom, Minister of Economic Affairs (later Finance), were Ambassadors in Delhi and Kuala Lumpur. Sunthorn had previously served in the Ministry of Education and as Chairman of the National Economic Council. Sawat Mahaphon, Minister of Agriculture, was also a civil servant (he was replaced, on his death later that year, by General Surajit).

The Government is frankly authoritarian. Article 17 of the Interim Constitution states in part: 'During the enforcement of the present Constitution, whenever the Prime Minister deems appropriate for the purpose of repressing or suppressing actions whether of internal or external origin which jeopardize the national security of the Throne or subvert or threaten law and order, the Prime Minister, by resolution of the Council of Ministers, is empowered to issue orders or take steps accordingly. Such orders or steps shall be considered legal.'*

---

* Summary execution, under Article 17, has occurred in about half a dozen cases of persons accused of arson, Communism and heroin ('999' and 'Lucky Strike') manufacture.

Marshal Sarit speaks to the public like a general addressing his troops. General Thanom, for his part, dismissed rumours that the Government would raise martial law as a 'New Year's Present' (1960) to the people: 'Other countries have had martial law for years. Nobody is suffering because of martial law. There is less crime than before.' The Prime Minister was even more curt (November 1961). Asked by a reporter whether it was not time that martial law was lifted, he replied: 'This is not yet the time. We still have to combat the narcotic drug trade (heroin). And there are also other problems.'

Previously, in July 1959, General Prapart had met some difficulty with the Bangkok Municipal Council, which had not approved a system of residential zones under the USOM (American aid) city plan. He was asked if the Council would be dissolved. 'Today, no,' the General replied, 'but tomorrow I am not sure. . . . Dissolving a Municipal Council is not as difficult as you think. I have already dissolved thirty in Thailand!'

The Constituent Assembly, appointed in February 1959 to draft a permanent Constitution, decided on November 10, 1960, by a vote of sixty-eight to twelve, that its members had no right to submit questionnaires to Cabinet Ministers on matters within their fields of responsibility. Marshal Sarit supported the views of a well-known lawyer that Assemblymen could not question Ministers. The Prime Minister added that the Assembly was only an advisory body and could not control the executive.

The Constituent Assembly agreed (September 1960) that a military court could try not only regular criminal cases during the period of martial law, but also any other cases assigned to it by the Supreme Commander of the Armed Forces (Marshal Sarit). The latter himself pointed out in a letter to the Minister of the Interior (June 11, 1960), that under normal court procedure there might not be sufficient evidence against suspected criminals or Communists, 'as the court must give the benefit of the doubt to the defendant'. However, 'in my position of responsibility for the whole nation, we should be more concerned over the welfare of the general public than over a small minority'.

This arbitrary use of power cannot but be a source of anxiety so long as martial law continues. All the same, there is a great improvement over the former regime. The Thanom Government pledged itself not to violate the constitutional immunity of Assemblymen during sessions. General Prapart said: 'We are trying to bring cleanliness where there has been dirtiness. We are not going to dirty things up again.' Marshal Sarit, who assumed the position of Acting Director-General of the Police Department in September 1959, declared: 'There is a lot to be done to improve the police force. . . . The police force has to be made more efficient and deserving of public trust.' Police throughout the country have been warned against abuses of authority. The Deputy Police Chief, Police General Prasert Ruchirawong, stated in August 1960 that police of some units 'arrested persons they hated or with whom they had quarrels or on whom they wished to take revenge, and then detained them as hooligans'. He added that this caused much trouble to innocent members of the public. Offending policemen would be severely punished.

A number of Communist suspects, mostly journalists, would be released because of lack of evidence, the Prime Minister reported in October 1959. But the 'political prisoners'—for reasons of security—are not yet reprieved. The Criminal Court admitted in July 1960 that it had no jurisdiction to consider the appeal of forty-nine Communist suspects, led by Thep, against illegal detention. The Court said it lay within the jurisdiction of the Military Court, because all were arrested and detained during martial law. The Criminal Court ruled in February 1961 that 121 Communist suspects had been legally detained under Revolutionary Announcement No. 12, which has the effect of a law. These suspects have been in prison, without trial, since October 1958.*

Marshal Sarit asserted that they 'had actually shown themselves to be Communists through activities, words, writings and journeys abroad to contact foreign Communists'. But Communists were clever. 'They know how to evade the law. It is

* Thep was formally charged in July 1962 in the Bangkok Military Court with membership of the Afro-Asian (People's) Solidarity Organization, considered to be a Communist organization. (Strictly, it is an odd mixture of neutralists and Communists, with its Secretariat in Cairo.) The police previously stated, in May, that fifty-two of the 121 suspects had been charged in court and fifteen released.

difficult to catch them with the evidence that the court would need to convict them. If we let them do as they please, without catching them, they would increase the threat to the nation and the people. . . . Because of this, orders were issued to arrest persons we were sure were Communists or pro-Communists or persons working for the Communists. These orders were issued with revolutionary powers. . . . Orders of the Revolutionary Party are the same as law.'

There are still frequent reports of arrests. In June 1960 the Prime Minister spoke of 'a great increase in Communist activities, chiefly carried out by the Chinese'. In July, two men were arrested, one a former monk, the other a villager in whose house eighteen Communist documents were found. Five printing offices in Bangkok were raided in August, and subversive documents found in four of them. (Two of the owners were also fortune-tellers.) Thirteen suspects from the South, arrested in November, included merchants, teachers, a village headman and a former police officer. Anti-Government leaflet ssigned by the 'Central Committee of the Thai Communist Party' were found near the capital, in Rajburi Province.

Over a hundred 'plotters' were arrested in the North-East in May 1961 and three months later the police were still seeking another hundred. The Minister of the Interior, General Prapart, charged that those arrested were spreading Communist, or at least 'anti-Government', propaganda in the villages, training picked men for guerrilla warfare and creating disturbances—in association with the Pathet Lao—in order to prepare the North-East for a Communist take-over. The plotters, he said, spoke of getting Russian and Chinese aid to develop the North-East. They promised villagers they would set up schools, give free schooling, and provide Soviet and Chinese tractors for collective farms. At the end of May a former deputy (from the Socialist Front) and another suspect were executed. In July two more deputies, including a former assistant Minister of Education, Fong Sittitharm, were arrested. An earlier plotter then confessed that Pridi, Kong Lae and Prince Souphanouvong were involved. Communists, the Minister of the Interior pointed out, were trying to get the North-Easterners to consider themselves as Laotians (the people of the North-East and of Laos speak the same dialect and are both known to Bangkok citizens as 'Lao') and were trying to effect a split between people and officials.

The 'treasonous plot', affirmed Marshal Sarit on Armed Forces Day (November 8, 1961, anniversary of the 1947 military coup against Pridi), 'was hatched with the support and collusion of the Communists from Laos who infiltrated to subvert the Thai nation. . . . One arrest by the police has by no means done away with all of them, many still remain and are still carrying on underground activities'. Communists, reported a Thai newspaper, *Chao Thai*, had been sending large numbers of weapons into the region; but the authorities had difficulty in routing them out because villagers seldom talked when interrogated for fear of reprisal. However, one reason for their 'separatism' is clear. Bangkok's radio transmitter is too weak to reach much of the North-East—especially the disaffected outlying provinces—and people listen instead to.Radio Peking or Radio Laos. Only in December 1961 was a transmitter finally established in the North-East.

That month a further ninety-five Communist suspects were arrested* in the North-East, most of them from the province of Nakorn Panom, bordering the Mekong, and from adjoining Sakon Nakorn. Some of the arrested men, according to police reports, received arms training in the Pathet Lao-held area around Mahaxay, just across the border. 'The plotters wanted to establish a beach-head at Nakorn Panom,' declared Police Major-General Pote Bekanond, returning from North-East operations on December 18th. 'Villagers in various parts of the province were recruited by persons sent by the Pathet Lao.' Local Thai recruits were said to be paid 200 baht a month but those with secondary education received about 2,000 baht (over £33 or $100). General Thanom later reported that a

* Thirty-eight suspects were arrested in central Thailand in February 1962. Suphanburi, north of Bangkok, was said to be the chief centre of subversion. A leader, Ruam Wongphan, confessed that he had studied at Peking for eight months in 1950 and a further year in Hong Kong. In 1958 he became a Communist Party member, recruiting 500 persons in Suphanburi and Lopburi Provinces. Six suspects told the police they were poor farmers, considerably in debt, and were 'taken in' by Communist promises of money, allocations of farm land and tractors for use on farms. Altogether 1,080 Communist suspects were arrested between October 1958 and June 1962 (according to the police), 420 of them tried, 186 released, 286 Vietnamese deported (with 6 to follow); 4 died in prison, 4 were executed and 3 escaped.

'Thai Exiles Association' had been formed in Communist-held Laos and that even certain Thai district officers had 'submitted to training for revolt by the Communists in Laos'. He added that army as well as police forces might have to be used for 'suppressive measures' in the North-East.

Suspicion and fear of Communism and official zeal to liquidate it sometimes lead to strange results. A serious case of arson, later traced to a merchant claiming insurance on over-insured property, occurred shortly after the Revolution. But the first report said: 'As a result of the investigation of the police and the Revolutionary Party, it was established beyond all doubt that the Taladploo fire was Communist-inspired. . . . The Communists are warned once and for all that if they still persist in their heinous offences against the security and welfare of the Thai people, they shall meet with reprisal unprecedented in Thai history.'*

The break-up of a notorious gangster and smuggling ring in Chonburi Province, in July 1959, was also hailed as a setback for Communism, later announced as 'not political in nature'. An alarming report of 'an international Communist con-spiracy' against Thailand was published by police and military investigators in June 1960, in these terms: evidence was received of 'agitation among students and a planned demon-stration on June 24th' (formerly 'Constitution Day'); 'Com-munists were infiltrating into ecclesiastical circles and attempt-ing to create dissension among monks'; and a bomb had been placed at the gate of the US Embassy.

As usual, it was discovered later that none of these activities —even the bomb—had much to do with Communism. The bomb was placed in protest against an American rice and wheat deal with India, which it was believed would undercut Thai exports. Education Ministry officials discovered that the student demonstrators were finishing higher vocational educa-tion and could not find jobs. The monks were dissatisfied at certain promotions within the hierarchy, following the death of the Lord Patriarch.

Thus intrigues and discontents have been blown up into Communist conspiracies, which either needlessly alarm the

---

* General Prapart reaffirmed (April 1962) that Communists 'plotting the step-by-step destruction of the country' were responsible for many up-country fires.

populace (as with the headlines about 'Chinese Reds' quoted by Sarit), or else render it apathetic—through constant repetition, leading nowhere—to real possibilities of danger. Reasons for over-sounding the alarm are partly internal, to vindicate the Revolution, and partly external, to attract more aid and sympathy from the United States. But motives go deeper. Beyond all calculations, military and police leaders' attitudes towards Communism are such that it is difficult for them to consider disturbances of any sort without springing to the conclusion that Communists are behind them.

'This shows that socialists eventually turn into Communists,' was the comment of the Prime Minister in July 1959 on documents alleging contacts between Communists and labour unions. 'Students should remain united,' said the Minister of Defence (also Rector of Thammasat University) in June 1960, 'to prevent trouble caused by a third hand.' The Minister of the Interior (also Rector of Chulalongkorn University) announced in March 1962 his plan to set up a 'university police corps' to protect property, direct traffic and 'maintain peace and order'. Such opinions come naturally to men of authority; but they have also been developed by the years of instruction in Free World foreign policy. ('Socialism is Communism, Neutralism is Immoral, Anti-Communism is Freedom.') The consequence is a distorted picture of the modern world and, what is worse, an unrealistic one. In any country there is the very difficult problem of reconciling civil liberty with the security of the State. There is no need to aggravate it by exaggerating the dangers of subversion.

Governments tend to support the State at the expense of individual liberty; it is the pressure of public opinion through newspapers, political parties, trade unions and other organizations which helps to preserve the balance. Without these safeguards the innocent, too, may suffer with the guilty. Given strong feelings against Communism, the military sense of security, awareness of the failure of the parliamentary system and the desire to press on with economic development, it is not surprising, however, that the present regime approaches democracy with extreme caution.

*   *   *

'Western democracy,' Marshal Sarit addressed the nation on the first Constitution Day (December 10th) after seizing power, 'is not such a system of government as could be adopted and put into operation immediately by all countries, regardless of the state of economic and political progress.' It was high time we learnt 'to adapt our democratic system to suit local needs and conditions'. A Constituent Assembly 'will be instituted to draft a new Constitution which will be more in keeping with the needs and conditions of the Thai people'. And more to the point: 'freedom *per se* will not contribute to the progress of the country. The exercise of freedom to introduce Communism into the country or to foment unrest and subversion after the fashion of the Communists is highly deleterious to the country and cannot be tolerated by the Revolutionary Party.'

Leaving aside the question of subversion, democracy as practised in the country was rather meaningless: During the big February 1957 election, wrote David A. Wilson and Herbert P. Phillips in *Far Eastern Survey*, August 1958, the authors informally, but systematically, asked a number of villagers, 'What is the purpose of the election?' More than half could not provide a direct answer, saying merely, 'It is the custom of the nation; when we are told to go and vote, we have to do so.' The minority that gave direct answers tended to repeat what they had been hearing on the radio or reading on campaign posters: 'To elect people to parliament who will represent us', or 'to elect representatives who will make laws for the country'. When asked to specify what they meant by 'represent' or 'make laws for the country', they replied in one of three ways: either they simply repeated what they had just said, or they admitted they did not know, or they continued in an equally vague vein—'to make laws for the country so that everybody will be happy and life will be comfortable'.

In a speech of October 1959 Marshal Sarit pointed out that democracy in Thailand had not worked successfully because it had been built from the top towards the base and not from the ground upward. He said there should first be a municipal government base from which to build up to a National Assembly and a Constitution. But economic action, rather than democracy, was essential if they were to keep abreast of advanced countries. 'Within six years, with economic development and educational improvement going along hand-in-hand, progress of the nation will be marked.'

And again, on Constitution Day, 1959: 'The constitutional form of government will endure only as long as the nation can maintain discipline. Without national discipline, freedom will be strained and twisted out of shape to serve individual and selfish purposes. . . . The reason why so much drastic action has been taken lately and why so many problems have been solved without any compromise is to accustom the Thai people to the rule of discipline. Once discipline prevails in all departments of the national life, it will become a solid basis on which an enduring constitutuent system may be built.'

The Constitutional Assembly itself had been appointed in February 1959. It was composed of 181 members of the armed forces and fifty-one civilians. The latter included scientists, scholars, legal experts, economists, press representatives, former prime ministers and ministers (two, at least of them, supporters of Phao and three of Pridi), but more than 90 per cent of the civilians were government officials.

Four committees were elected at the end of March 1961 to start work on drafting the Constitution. The Prime Minister made clear to the members that they were not to consider themselves bound to favour the Government's line of thought or action and told them not to be deterred 'from acting independently and in all good faith by the fear of incurring the Revolutionary Party's or my own displeasure. . . .' To act in a 'thorough and broad-minded' way, a 'Public Opinion Appraisal Committee' would present to the Drafting Committee 'a faithful assessment of the attitudes of various segments of the population', which 'would be tantamount to actual public participation'.* Marshal Sarit went on:

'You will probably be working in two stages, that is to say you will first study the constitutions of eighty countries available

* Almost half the members of the various committees are senior officers. Among the twenty-one members of the Public Opinion Appraisal Committee are also journalists, including Kukrit, business men and the head of the tourist organization. General Thanom and Prince Wan, the two Deputy Premiers, are on the Drafting Committee. General Prapart is on the Agenda Committee. Also on the fifteen-member Drafting Committee is Luang Vichit Vadhakarn, one of the Prime Minister's chief advisers and probably the inspiration for the address that follows.

to acquire an expert knowledge of the constitutions. You will then come to the second phase, that of working out, through the process of assimilation and comparison or even pure invention, whatever is suited to the conditions of Thailand and the mentality of the Thai people. . . .

'Enquiry into foreign practices would only provide points of reference and not inordinately influence our thinking. . . . All theories must be put to the test from time to time and in some cases are found faulty. . . . Even a popular concept such as democracy is differently defined. Even in modern times electoral procedure and suffrage also vary from country to country. Surprisingly enough, women are still denied suffrage in some countries regarded as paragons of democracy. . . . This clearly testifies to the relativity of principles and theories. The point I wish to make is that we need not feel diffident about inventing something outright for our own use so long as we are certain it is suitable for our country. . . .

'The system of checks and balances puts a curb on any wanton or arbitrary exercise of power. This is the essence of the constitutional regime. In themselves these checks and balances are good but they must be fairly and honestly used. There must be effective safeguards against using the Constitution to clog the progress of the nation, destroy others or advance personal prestige or interest. Power must entail responsibility. This is the view that I vigorously maintain. . . . The last thing I would like to mention is that while the Constituent Assembly is working on the Constitution, the Government and myself will proceed with the work of strengthening the foundations of the constitutional regime, that is to say, we shall go ahead with our work of educational and economic development. . . . I wish to see that enough progress has materialized to warrant the belief that the good work will not be undone by the new National Assembly convened by virtue of the new Constitution.'

In fact drafting proceeds in a leisurely way. The Constituent Assembly first took up the question of the name of the country, resolving the point in favour of Thailand rather than Siam a month later. In August a new problem, the status of the King, presented itself. It was later agreed that the King would appoint the Cabinet, the latter stating its policies to the Assembly, but not requiring a vote of confidence by the

Assembly (September 21st); Cabinet Ministers should not be members of the Assembly (October 5th): the term of the Cabinet should be the same as that of the Assembly; the King can dissolve the Assembly, deputies may question Cabinet Ministers and they may hold a general debate on the Government without taking a vote (October 19th); if they wish they may require a vote of confidence (November 16th). The Prime Minister, through the King, can dismiss a Cabinet Minister (approved by sixty votes to thirty-six, November 30, 1961).*

Unfortunately, this is all rather academic. For the Prime Minister had already stated his belief, according to 'authoritative sources' (April 27, 1961), that the draft Constitution should provide for general elections to take place: (i) five years after the promulgation of the Constitution; or (ii) after completion of the present economic development plans; or (iii) when political conditions are considered stable and the time appropriate for elections to be held. The Prime Minister was said to have wished the Constitution to be completed by the end of the year, but this was denied two days later. 'No one can predict,' reported the Office of the Prime Minister, 'exactly when the Constitution will be fully drafted.'

Perhaps the foremost theorist of the new order is Thanat Khoman, the Foreign Minister. 'While certain countries can justly be proud that their Government is under civilian control,' he stated in August 1958 (when still Thai Ambassador in Washington), 'it does not necessarily follow that each and every nation must immediately achieve their ultimate political perfection without regard to prevailing circumstances, political as well as economic and educational. . . . All this, to be realistic, has to depend on various factors such as unstable political conditions due to economic disturbances or even to external pressure.' He added that 'democracy certainly does exist in Thailand' in the sense of civil rights carefully observed by constituted authorities, freedom of speech and especially of the

* There is to be an elected House of Representatives and an appointed Senate, it was decided, by 118 votes to 4 (February 22, 1962). The upper house, according to speakers, would 'sift and scrutinize Bills more carefully' and prevent 'easy Communist infiltration into the Assembly'. A dissentient, however, approved one (elected) chamber only so that 'people who have votes can control the Government, which is the core of democracy'. The powers of the appointed Senate remain to be seen.

press, and the absence of discrimination against people for arbitrary reasons.

In a further address, in March 1959, he argued that immature democracy was itself to blame for the instability of Thai political life:

'How can a free press play its role in voicing the views of the public if it is not fully aware of its responsibility, and when it mistook its own misguided or selfish view as the opinion of the masses? How can representative government function if those who are elected to represent the people in the National Assembly forget the interest of the country as a whole and pursue only their selfish gains? More particularly, how can the electorate hope to choose representatives worthy of their trust if it is hardly able to distinguish between promises of an election campaign and the genuine determination to carry out a national programme and to uphold political ideals?'

Should Thailand try once more to 'revamp the imported institutions, adapt them to our needs and replant them with the hope that they will take root and prosper?' In his own view, 'it is preferable to fall back on ourselves . . . and forget about these institutions for a time. It is immaterial if in this process some voices from abroad may clamour that democracy experiences a setback in Asia. . . . It is of no avail to try to ape those who, after all, are different from us in many respects.'

And here (as previously cited) is his reply to the West: 'If we look back at our national history, we can very well see that this country works better and prospers under an authority around which all elements of the nation can rally. On the contrary, the dark pages of our history show that whenever such an authority is lacking and dispersal elements had their play, the nation was plunged into one disaster after another. . . . The authority that this country needs will be beneficial if it can spur national enthusiasm into working as a team towards the betterment of our nation. . . .'

This is a plea for benevolent authority, not democracy—despite the hope that 'authority will not trespass its proper limits', because of 'the store of democratic faith in our traditions'. It is, in fact, the case against democracy—as it was practised in Thailand. But there *is* a case for democracy.

PROBLEMS OF ASIAN DEMOCRACY

Despite the failure, and the downfall, of democratic institutions over much of the world, there is a case for democracy. It rests on the assumption, as the present Lord Lindsay has said, that a 'process of discussion and study of the evidence will tend to produce a concensus of opinion about what is the right thing to do'.

This is probably true of the 'concensus of opinion' but not necessarily of the 'right thing'. There is no certainty that a group of people (rather than one person) will know the right answer to a political problem. The group may be more swayed by mass emotions than the individual. But the group know their own problems more than any one individual can do; they know 'where the shoe pinches'.

Democracy brings a variety of points of view to bear; for however wise or benevolent a king or dictator may be (though examples have been none too conspicuous), their decisions remain arbitrary. The clash of informed opinion is more likely to lead to reasonable solutions. Dictators are notoriously unwilling to accept opinions contrary to their own: it is they who dictate. Yet conflicts of opinion may also lead to deadlock; for the more that is known of a problem the more difficult it becomes to act. Thinking breeds complexity. Action requires simplicity—a 'clear-cut' case. Leadership *and* advice are necessary: they are more often found to be combined in democracies than in dictatorships.

From advice springs consent. People are more likely to accept what is to be done—and what they, the people, must do—if it is based on the advice of those that they, or at least the majority of them, have chosen. Persuasion is better than force. In fact, the use of force is a confession of failure. No one seriously suggests that force provides a sensible, or lasting, solution to problems: the winner is stronger, not necessarily more 'right'.

It is fashionable to argue, nevertheless (as Guy Wint and other commentators have done), that democratic institutions do not matter, provided there is legal integrity, personal freedom and a free expression of opinion. But what is to keep all these going without the support of democratic institutions, or the pressure of public opinion? On the freedom of politics, which means the free choice of political parties, all other freedoms ultimately depend.

The case against democracy—and it is a strong case over much of the world, particularly in Asia—is really the case against the *abuses* of democracy. It may be that democracy divides, and introduces bitter party conflict, but the division in politics also reflects an existing social division; instead of being concealed, it is brought into the open. Democracy brings undesirable personalities into politics, but so does any other system of rule. Even government by mediocrity may be preferable to the alternation of benevolence and tyranny produced by hereditary government (monarchy) or force (dictatorship). Democracy gives politics an urban bias and a bias against the peasantry. This is natural enough: politics are an urban feature, though democracy itself, as 'self-government,' is characteristic of the village. Political issues indeed more directly concern the towns, but where they do affect the country rural interests have been known to defend their own.

A more fundamental case, at least in Asia, is the traditional opposition to, or lack of understanding of, argument and division. The idea of forcing a decision, of a majority excluding the minority, is widely distrusted. Asian village traditions favour the 'sense of the meeting'. Ideally, there is no question of obstruction or opposition in village life; every decision is reached through discussion and general agreement. This age-old type of village democracy, its defenders claim, suits Asian needs and circumstances better than the Western type of democracy.

There are two objections to this. First, the tradition itself has been dying out over much of Asia. 'Mutual help' works when villagers co-operate to build each other a house or harvest the paddy, but it is unsuited to more complex problems. Secondly, it has always been limited to the village itself. Kings or chiefs ruled absolutely from the centre and their decisions could (and often did) plunge the country into war and devastation.

This is the crux of the matter. Local self-government is, and has always been, possible, but can it be carried out on a nationwide scale? The problem is how to link the 'direct democracies' of villages and towns with the machinery of government at the centre. The Western solution is representative democracy, where the people choose their representatives to rule—i.e. control the administration—in their name. It is on the choice of these representatives and their integrity and efficiency that the system stands or falls. Yet it took the best part of a century to develop the full mechanism of democracy in Britain and hundreds of years of 'preparation' before that.

Is it possible therefore to found institutions of democracy in Asia, to face the most bitter and intractable of problems, almost unprepared (by centuries of absolutism), and expect them to succeed all at once?

A Burmese scholar, Maung Maung Gyi, writing in the *Nation* of Rangoon, concedes that the 'people, by and large, are still dominated by the authoritarian view and habits of the old pre-British days'. Indeed throughout Asia, external restraints on a man of authority were felt to be incongruous. 'All that could be expected of him was to possess the six attributes of a true leader, namely, patience, vigilance, assiduity, critical faculty, sympathy and sagacity or wisdom, and act accordingly.' As for the people, their 'intense desire' was to 'avoid anything to do with government'. They believed 'that government was an evil, that oppression and misrule were natural, that it was futile to stand up against the Government even on legitimate grounds, that the Government was not the concern of the people, that the Government will take care of anything ... that security in office depended upon the pleasure of the superior and therefore one's duty was to please one's superior. ...'

The result of absolutism of the few is apathy among the many, and apathy prevents any vigorous effort being made, unless by compulsion, to meet modern problems. It is still democracy, as the President of Pakistan has observed (in the July 1960 issue of *Foreign Affairs*), that provides the 'only healthy and dignified way for arousing the willing co-operation of people and harnessing it to a sustained national endeavour'. The pre-requisites of democracy are fourfold. 'It should be simple to understand, easy to work and cheap to sustain. It should put to the voter only such questions as he can answer in

H

the light of his own personal knowledge and understanding without external prompting. It should ensure the effective participation of all citizens in the affairs of the country up to the level of their mental horizon and intellectual calibre. It should be able to produce reasonably strong and stable government.'

This is an effective guide to action. The need, admittedly greater where population presses heavily on resources, as in countries like India, Pakistan, Indonesia and China, is to rouse the people. Democracy, in the first three cases, thus becomes a function of national development. Its failure to function in Pakistan, as in Nationalist China, presented the alternative of dictatorship or chaos. Indonesia, so far, hovers between them. Pakistan, under Ayub Khan, now settles for 'basic democracies' —local democracy, which diminishes rapidly from the (self-governing) village to the (largely nominated) district and provincial councils. Here they meet the same problem of linking—and reconciling—village democracy and central administration.*

China relies on inspiration and force, closely controlled and organized by the Communist Party. India on persuasion and example—notably in rural community development, which has, however, made little progress against traditional obstacles of lack of initiative and class conflict (between labourers, tenant farmers, money-lenders and landowners). In India, too, the role of leadership provided by the Congress Party has sadly disintegrated into communal separatism, political faction and personal intrigue.

It is still a question, in the democracies as under Communism, of *effective* government. Problems of poverty, over-population, illiteracy, unemployment and disease must be solved. Premature or pseudo democracy is worse than useless if it fails to do so; it only prejudices future possibilities. A gradual approach, constantly extending the scope of self-government (with real

* There is a further drawback to local self-government. Villages and towns-people may indeed know their own problems, but they are rarely sufficiently 'taken' with constitutions (in any country) to deal with them in this way. Thus the system tends to fall into the hands of cliques, either wealthy or subversive, who use it for their own ends. Perhaps only the knowledge that local councils do have full powers to deal with their own problems—and are not checked or suppressed whenever they become 'difficult'—will really ensure participation by the people.

financial powers), is the surest method. Gradually under-standing grows, and with it, responsibility. But the greatest responsibility lies with the national leadership, of whatever form, to promote and encourage democracy eventually to replace it.

CHAPTER 6

FOREIGN AFFAIRS

Thai tribesmen migrated from China, about a thousand years ago, in three waves. To the west, they settled in the hills and forests of upper Burma; to the east, in the still more difficult country along the banks of the Mekong. The first called themselves Shan, the second Lao. Only the third wave, between the Shan and Lao tribes, had the good fortune to penetrate the upper reaches of the tributaries of the Menam Chaophraya, and then to advance along the great river itself into the fertile plain and down to the sea. They were the ancestors of the present Thais.

NEIGHBOURS

The Shans were one of five or six diverse elements in Burma: Burmans proper, settled along the Irrawaddy valley; Mons, who had formed an ancient and civilized kingdom in the south-east; the Karen tribes in the east; and various others. The Laos shared their isolated existence with Thai, Miao, Kha and numerous small tribes. The Thais, too, faced the Mon people, whom they rapidly dispossessed in the north, and then confronted the outposts of the great Khmer Empire. From the twelfth to the fifteenth century—when the Thais occupied Angkor and drove the Khmer kings to found a new capital— there were incessant battles and skirmishes. The Thais were continually being reinforced by their fellows from China and their vigour and strength proved too much for the Khmers, already declining from their days of glory. Khmers (Cambodians), Burmese, Mons, Laos and later Vietnamese—these are the elements affecting Thai foreign policy for the next three hundred years.

Thailand (Siam) was a fairly united country, smaller than

Burma, and bigger than Cambodia. So long as the Burmese kings were weak, or the country was divided into strong Mon or Shan states, Siam could hold its own. But with powerful kings, uniting the whole of Burma under one authority, Siam suffered repeated invasions and twice her capital, Ayuthaya, was seized and large numbers of Thais led captive to Burma. Only under King Naresuen (a contemporary of Queen Elizabeth of England) were the Burmese decisively repelled and the battle carried far into Burma. The king, mounted on elephantback, in single combat slew the Crown Prince of Burma.

For Cambodia the situation was reversed. The Thais were ever defeating the Khmers, annexing parts of their territory or claiming suzerainty over the whole. Just as in Western Europe the Scots took advantage of wars between England and France to regain their independence and attack the English, so the Cambodians waited to invade until Siam was hard pressed by the Burmese. Cambodia, however, lay between two fires: to the east were the able and aggressive Vietnamese who had already swallowed up one kingdom—Champa, once a rival of Angkor—and now contested Cambodia with the Thais. As for Laos, the kingdoms of Vientiane and Luang Prabang were sometimes independent, sometimes tributary to Burma (as was most of Northern Siam), sometimes to Siam.

Contacts with Europe started with Portuguese, early in the sixteenth century, and Dutch, English and French traders a century later. Towards the end of that century the British East India Company was well established in India, the Dutch in Indonesia and the French, also in India, sought further expansion in Siam. Their venture in Siam, partly religious, partly imperial, ended in disaster. French missionaries thereupon moved to Vietnam (replacing Chinese characters with the Latin alphabet) and their efforts sowed the seeds of French influence, and eventually 'protection', in later years.

In the nineteenth century most of Asia came under European domination. The British defeated the Burmese Kingdom in 1824 and the Chinese Empire in 1839—the Opium War. These were shattering events: lower Burma was annexed to the British Empire and the Burmese threat to Siam was ended once and for all, only fifty years after the greatest Burmese triumph, the capture and sack of Ayuthaya. The kings of Siam recognized the might of Britain, as the last Burmese king, to his cost, still failed to do. They relinquished their oriental disdain in the face of Western barbarism (as many European customs seemed to them to be) and came to terms with the new Empire.

By the end of the last century and up to the outbreak of the Second World War, Britain ruled India, the whole of Burma, Malaya and North Borneo; France ruled, under protectorates, Laos, Cambodia and Vietnam; the Netherlands, Indonesia. China in decay granted humiliating concessions to many of the European powers and so did Siam. The extraordinary success of the Japanese after Pearl Harbor gave the death-blow to European colonization; but the Japanese by their brutality and arrogance alienated the sympathies of the nationalist leaders. Sukarno, Aung San and Ho Chi Minh, each supreme in his own country, faced very different prospects. Thailand, still angered with the French for their seizure of Laos and expansion of Cambodia, supported these nationalist movements. (Ho Chi Minh before the war was for a short time an exile in Bangkok). Whereas the British yielded to the demand for independence, the Dutch tried to resist it and the French fought it.

Even though South-East Asia has regained its freedom, nationalism remains a powerful and destructive force. Indonesian hostility to the Dutch is inconceivable without realizing the passion of their demand, however unjustified, for West Irian. So is China's fury with America for 'occupying' Taiwan. So are the anger, fear and suspicion aroused by disputes between Thailand and Cambodia and Cambodia and Vietnam.

There are unifying factors. A common source of culture, from India—except for Vietnam, which follows China—is one of them. The Buddhist religion is another. Burma, Thailand, Laos and Cambodia are all countries of Theravada Buddhism. But Malaya and Indonesia are Moslem; the Philippines, Christian; and Vietnam, like old China, is a repository of beliefs, Buddhist, Confucian, Taoist, all acceptable but none strongly held. (The Chinese are practical people and do not greatly concern themselves with other-worldly speculation.) Buddhism, if it mitigates the strife in Laos, also has to its credit a delightful diplomatic accord between Thailand and Burma.* Some years ago a Burmese plane, attacking rebels, bombed a

* Hugh Tinker writing on U Nu in *Pacific Affairs*, June 1957.

Thai village by mistake. U Nu, the Burmese Prime Minister (and a devoted Buddhist), hastened to apologize. Not at all, replied Marshal Pibun, his Thai counterpart. Nu offered compensation: Pibun returned it with thanks. The Burmese finally gave a cheque for use in works of merit in Thailand.

Causes of disunity in South-East Asia are varied. Firstly, the borders are often poorly defined. Secondly, central governments have not the authority to control outlying populations, who are accustomed to smuggle or raid across frontiers with impunity. Thirdly, populations are mixed: large numbers of Cambodians live in Cochin-China (South Vietnam) and many Vietnamese in Cambodia (a third of the population of Phnom-Penh is Vietnamese, another third Chinese); many Khmers live in Thailand, and Thais in Cambodia; Karens spread over from Burma into Thailand and other hill tribes roam, unconscious of frontiers, in these countries as in Laos, North Vietnam and South-West China. Fourthly, the legacy of the past, the pride in past civilizations (notably in Cambodia), and the humiliation and fear of past defeats. And finally, ideology, whether Communism, neutralism, or commitment to the West, which all reinforce national desire and traditional prejudice. The path to unity in South-East Asia is long and hard.

PROBLEMS

Thailand's present, if not past, relations are at their best with Burma, at their worst with Cambodia. Burma, traditionally the powerful oppressor, was subjected to colonialism and has been ravaged by the civil strife of Communists, Karens, certain Shans and ex-Kuomintang Chinese. Thailand, spared foreign domination and internal unrest, has drawn level, perhaps ahead. But Cambodia, with a population one-fifth that of Thailand, still fears her past overlord, who only twenty years ago regained four provinces and yielded them with reluctance. With deeply-felt ideological differences, mixed border populations and extreme suspicion on both sides, only a spark was needed to cause an explosion.

The spark was a tenth-century temple built on a spur overlooking Cambodia, with a sheer drop of hundreds of feet below.

Hard to reach from Thailand—a train journey of many hours from Bangkok, then by bus or jeep for four hours and finally on foot—it is virtually inaccessible from Cambodia. Few people, either Thai or Cambodian, were interested. But this temple, *Khao Phra Viharn*, geographically Thai, culturally Khmer, was clumsily located within the Cambodian frontier as drawn by the French who negotiated Thailand's cession of four provinces to Cambodia early this century. The question of ownership remained latent many years. Then, with Cambodian independence, Prince Sihanouk revived the claims of the Khmers.

Negotiations took place, at the highest level, in August 1958. The obvious solution was suggested by General Thanom, then Prime Minister, who said he might be willing to agree to 'joint administration'. This was met by storms of protests from Thai nationalists. Thanom was compelled to retract: '*Khao Phra Viharn* is 100 per cent Thai', but facilities to Cambodian visitors would be offered. Early in September, a mob of several thousands started marching on the Cambodian Embassy in Bangkok after listening to inflammatory demands for the return of the former Thai territories. The Minister of the Interior, General Prapart, came out in his sports shirt to praise the '100 per cent loyalty' of the demonstrators, but he urged them to disperse. Instead they marched right on and 'truncheon-wielding police, water-spraying firemen and rifle-toting military policemen' fought 'screaming, bottle-and-brick throwing, plank-board swinging rioters in a two-hour battle', as the *Bangkok Post* reported.

Now demonstrations are unusual in Bangkok (they are prohibited at the moment); the force and fury of this one indicates the strength of feeling aroused. But this was not the end of the affair. In November 1958, Cambodian police arrested thirty-two Thai villagers on a charge of rustling cattle in Cambodia. Thailand claimed they were kidnapped (later it was thought they might have been 'tricked' into crossing the border). Cambodia withdrew her Ambassador and Thailand closed the border (thereby seriously inconveniencing American tourists wishing to visit Angkor). 'Cambodia,' *Siam Rath* alleged, 'started its campaign of intimidation against Thailand with the extending of recognition to Red China (in July). . . . This gave opportunities for Red China to station armed forces in Cambodia.' Officials of the Thai Ministry of the Interior, however, thought Cambodia was deliberately trying to provoke Thailand into what might look like aggression, in order to secure aid and sympathy from the outside world. Fortunately both countries accepted mediation by a United Nations official and, after several months, diplomatic relations were restored. The 'newspaper war', conducted with virulence on both sides, was temporarily ended by an agreement at New York in December 1960.

Ten months later the dispute flared up again. This time there were no immediate causes but a wider international entanglement. Prince Sihanouk, speaking in Tokyo early in October 1961, suggested that the 'opposition of unpopular and corrupt men and dictatorships of the "right" against dictatorships of the "left" ' was not the best means of defence against Communism. Cambodia herself, the Prince added gratuitously, 'has to fight not so much against Communism, as against her pro-Western neighbours'. Yet he denied reports from Thailand and South Vietnam that his country was being used as a base by Communist guerrillas fighting in, or infiltrating, Vietnam. (His denial was evidently confirmed, later.) But the Thai Prime Minister, prompted, some say, by Luang Vichit (an extreme nationalist of former years), denounced 'violent accusatory attacks' by the 'head of a certain country', who 'constantly makes himself out as an enemy of our country'. Marshal Sarit indicated, for good measure, the 'existence of a plan making his country (Cambodia) a springboard for launching attacks on neighbouring countries by Communist armed forces'.

Greatly excited, the Prince in turn (October 23rd) accused Thailand of seeking a 'marvellous pretext' for rushing to the aid of South Vietnam by sending a 'punitive expedition' against Cambodia. Thai neighbours 'since the fifteenth century,' he declared, 'have never ceased to wish to conquer our country, to enslave our race.' The Prince severed diplomatic relations with Thailand. Thailand next day closed the border; but 'we have no aggressive plans against Cambodia', said General Thanom. The Thai Ministry of Foreign Affairs issued a statement that the 'Cambodian press and radio never ceased engaging in campaigns of polemics and attacks against this country. . . .' Cambodian citizens started digging trenches in Phnom-Penh.

Peking was delighted at the opportunity to demonstrate China's 'firm support' for Cambodia's 'just stand . . . towards the outrageous provocation of US imperialism and its lackeys'. In fact, America's unofficial reaction was to regret this breach between the two countries at a time of increasing common danger from outside—at a time, moreover, when Prince Sihanouk had been taking action against incursions by Viet Cong guerrillas and against local Communist activities in Cambodia. Aggrieved, the Thai Ministry of Foreign Affairs complained (November 7th) that if friends 'are unable to show their sympathy', they should at least be impartial; they should not appear to support 'Cambodia, the wrongdoer' at the expense of 'Thailand, the innocent victim'. Since then, a more dignified silence has prevailed.*

Thailand's relations with Cambodia are an extreme case, and one that both sides have been trying, at times, to solve. But they illustrate the conditions that exist to influence the susceptibilities and suspicions of newly independent nations. Even with Malaya, where official relations are excellent and international policy coincides†—both countries are co-operating in the fight against the remaining Communist terrorists on the Thai-Malayan frontier—there is an obstacle: the Moslem, Malay-speaking inhabitants of South Thailand, whom the irredentist, Pan-Moslem Islamic Party in Malaya—as well as the Communist Party—is continually trying to stir up. But Thailand has promised not to interfere with the religious practices of this region. In fact, so long as the Alliance Government under Tunku Abdul Rahman remains in power in Malaya, there should be little to fear.

Karen and KMT rebels provide the irritant with Burma, whose normal relations with Thailand are good, despite the bitter experience of the past and the difference in international

---

* In June 1962, Cambodia's claim to the ruined temple of *Khao Phra Viharn* was accepted, on a technicality, by the International Court of Justice. Despite the fighting words of Generals Thanom and Prapart and an extraordinary outburst by Thanat, the Prime Minister, on royal advice, wisely decided to comply.

† Malaya, Thailand and the Philippines are joint signatories of ASA, the Association of South-east Asia for economic and cultural co-operation, founded in Bangkok in July 1961.

outlook. (The Burmese Embassy in Phnom-Penh represented Thailand during the break with Cambodia.) The lesser problem is that of the Karens who sought refuge in Thai frontier areas during their revolt against the Burmese Government. These Karens have in no way been hindered, and in certain cases have been aided, in supplying assistance to their fellow rebels in Burma.* The Karens, however, made a fatal error in May 1960. They attacked two Thai border towns, supposedly (the Burmese claim) because they were double-crossed over supplies. By this action, they have brought both Burmese and Thai forces together in joint operations against them.

The ex-KMT guerrillas are, or rather were, a far graver threat to international relations. Remnants of the Nationalist Chinese forces driven out of Yunnan, for years they have plagued the Burmese, at one time seizing large tracts of the Shan States. It was only with the utmost difficulty that the Burmese prevailed on the United States—after repeated protests in the United Nations—to airlift about half of them to Taiwan. The rest remained almost unassailable in the wild tangled regions near Thailand, comfortably organizing an opium-smuggling route, and assisted, from time to time, with arms and food supplied by Taiwan. It is an open secret that these supplies came through Thailand. Marshal Pibun announced in November 1956 that a KMT organization in Thailand was soliciting donations for funds, firearms and other supplies to the Chinese guerrillas in Burma. 'The KMT causes too much trouble,' he declared. 'They also trade in opium and cause Thailand to be blamed in the United Nations.'

The climax came in February 1961, when three Burmese fighters shot down a Nationalist Chinese aircraft dropping supplies to KMT troops in Burma. The plane fell just inside Thai territory. Another Chinese aircraft mistakenly dropped supplies to an outpost of the KMT over-run in a recent offensive by the Burma Army: these supplies included arms and ammunition from Taiwan, with American markings. The Thais, anxious to

* It is fair to add that Brigadier Aung Gyi of the Revolutionary Council in Burma publicly thanked the Thai Government early in March 1962 for preventing arms and supplies reaching the numerous Shan insurgents in Burma. Marshal Sarit commented that 'Thailand and Burma are very good friends and we are not going to get ourselves involved over the Shan States'.

shield Nationalist China, refused to disclose any details about the crashed plane. But it was too late. The new American Administration evidently feared that KMT troops driven out of Burma into Laos (and northern Thailand) might provoke Communist China's intervention. A hasty airlift was organized and in a matter of days most of the guerrillas were gone.

Refugees, of another persuasion, have also caused trouble for Thailand. These are Vietnamese, up to seventy thousand of them, who fled to North-East Thailand during the war against France. They are ardent supporters of Ho Chi Minh (his portrait hangs openly in their houses) and they are closely organized by Vietminh agents. Sixty Vietnamese leaders arrested in November 1958 were said to have been training refugees in guerrilla warfare. 'The training was chiefly in effective use of sharp bamboo poles as weapons, the way in which Vietminh guerrillas had fought in Vietnam,' explained a Thai police officer. As late as January 1961, Vietnamese refugees were reported holding secret shooting practices in the jungle near Laos. The danger, in the event of an invasion from North Vietnam, is that these refugees will sabotage Thai resistance in the strategic provinces bordering Laos.

Documents seized in June 1959 revealed that the Vietnamese community was being widely exploited by the Vietminh. Vietnamese settlers were using their industry and technical knowledge—they even outbid the Chinese—to penetrate the Thai armed forces and officials. Police discovered, according to a special report in the *Bangkok World*, that the Vietnamese had wormed their way into every sensitive post in their areas. Mechanics would save Thai officers and men the trouble of bringing in radios or cars, and willingly went into police and army compounds to do jobs. Soldiers were delighted to find that, not only did the Vietnamese do their washing better and cheaper, but they would come all the way out to the barracks to collect and deliver. 'In this way the Vietnamese were able easily to keep a constant watch on the activities of the military or police and even occasionally to obtain classified information.'

Repatriation to North Vietnam was the obvious solution and the Thais were delighted to reach an agreement, despite protests from the South, with the North Vietnam Red Cross.

By the end of 1961 about twenty-eight thousand Vietnamese had been evacuated from the country.

ALLIES

'The traditional foreign policy of Siam,' states Sir Josiah Crosby, 'has been one of studied neutrality.' She maintained a 'nice balance' between the great powers. Thai statesmen were past masters in playing off two countries against one another. 'No patriotic Siamese of reasonable intelligence would have thought of advocating any other line of foreign policy for his country. . . .' Then came the Japanese invasion, the British withdrawal from Malaya and Burma, the fall of Singapore. As Sir Josiah observes: 'The military system of which some of her (Thai) leaders had been so proud had absorbed a huge proportion of the national income, yet in the end it was powerless to preserve the neutrality and independence of the country, and it had degenerated previously into an instrument by which the new-born urge to democracy was treacherously suppressed.'

Neutrality—leaving aside the question of democracy—was not enough. Thailand under Pibun sided with the Japanese; 'Siam' under Pridi (he restored the old name) with the Allies; Thailand, again under Pibun, chiefly with the Americans. In 1950, in commitment to the anti-Communist cause, Pibun signed a treaty of military and economic aid with the United States. Thailand became one of the three Asian members of SEATO—with Pakistan and the Philippines—four years later.

Now this commitment, while reassuring to the security of the country—and, of course, to that of the military-police regime—aroused some uneasiness. It appeared to go too far, it left Thailand without much freedom to manoeuvre and she was regarded, by other nations, as merely a camp-follower of the Americans. In 1955 the Bandung Conference appeared to relax tensions. Chou En-lai, suave and benign, made an excellent impression on Asian delegates. In Thailand, internal restrictions on the Chinese were removed. The situation had evolved and Thai policy evolved with it.

On the surface, the Pibun Government maintained its policy of commitment; beneath it, devious currents of opinion were set in play. The Government, of course, was not responsible for what newspapers, politicians or trade unionists had to say. This was all the more plausible because in 1956 Pibun went on his world tour to discover democracy (and free speech) in England and America. He said he was anxious to put them into practice on his return.

This technique, employed to some extent by most governments, was a peace-time variant of the 'Pibun Songgram system', tried out in Thailand against the Japanese. 'Using this system,' General Phao had explained to provincial governors (in case of an enemy invasion), 'the governor should apparently co-operate with the enemy during the day but set up an underground movement to fight the enemy, especially during the night'. In this way, Phao said, he would prevent the enemy from oppressing the people.

Basically the Pibun regime stood by the alliance with the West. But the unofficial ventures—openings to the left— allowed a certain form of expression to public opinion, thus releasing some of the internal pressures on the regime; at the same time, they helped to avert the wrath of Communist powers and provided a means of reassurance for the future.

This 'system', opportune for a small country which could not defend itself alone, nor foretell the changes to come, aroused some disquiet in America. The *New York Times* alleged that important Thai newspapers, belonging to the leaders of the country, or under their influence, were publishing articles 'against the interests of the Free World'—and particularly the United States. The Government replied that Pibun and Phao had nothing to do with the operation of any newspaper. 'Publication of opinions by various newspapers,' it blandly declared, 'is a right and a freedom of the press with which the Government is not in a position to interfere.'

The Communists, Pibun went on, had ceased aggression, but they are 'now trying to be friends, to trade, to work underground, to come and sleep in bed with us'. The people of Thailand will never go Communist, he added reassuringly, but 'I quite agree that a mild sort of socialism may be good for Thailand'. Pibun at this time (it was shortly before elections) pledged himself to consider three trade union requests. Trade unions had recently been legalized. The requests were firstly that Thailand should be a free country, and not tied to a foreign country's policy. Secondly, that there should be free trade with all countries in the world, and the use of Thailand as a military base by foreign countries banned. Thirdly, that the Anti-Communist Act should be abrogated since labourers were afraid of this Act being used to hamper their labour movement.

Requests soon turned into demands. 'Thailand is not an American colony,' proclaimed May Day banners. 'Wipe out wicked imperialist culture', 'Abrogate the Anti-Communist Act', 'Adopt neutralist policy, Quit SEATO', 'We condemn Capitalist Association', and so on. 'Is the Pibun Government going left?', queried Khuang, the Democratic leader. 'It is dangerous stepping in two boats. If it is expertly done it is all right, but if it is not, it is dangerous.'

The Government was in fact precarious. Wild rumours of *coups* were denied: this was June 1957, during the last throes of a regime which had endured nearly ten years. Thailand would stick to the free democracies, Pibun asserted, but if an accurate measurement of public opinion approved neutrality, they would have to follow it: 'who dares go against public opinion?' Even Marshal Sarit, after the flight of Pibun and Phao in September, felt compelled to observe: 'I feel we should have an independent foreign policy, following in the footsteps of none.'

So much for the past. The present Government is once more strictly anti-Communist: trade with China is banned, no delegations there are permitted. But whereas Pibun, in his stabler moments, was in tune with the State Department, the situation has changed. American policy has evolved, notably in its treatment of neutrals, and it is now Thailand and other former 'Satellites' that are in danger of being left behind.*

American aid is an example. Such aid is deservedly popular, though military assistance lacks such appeal. But strange forms of aid from the past also occasionally come to light. The mysterious 'South-East Asia Supply Corporation', connected with the American Central Intelligence Agency, helped finance

---

* 'Our unfulfilled task,' says President Kennedy, 'is to demonstrate to the entire world that man's unsatisfied aspirations for economic progress and social justice can best be achieved by free men working within a framework of democratic institutions.'—March 13, 1961.

General Phao in his task of 'combatting subversion'; in fact, as might have been imagined, these funds became 'private, secret aid solely for General Phao', so his successor complained. Further unhappiness is caused—but for entirely opposite reasons—by the amount of American aid given to neutrals, at the expense, so the Thais see it, of 'staunch SEATO allies like Thailand'.*

'There is great disappointment in high Thai official circles over American aid allotments for the current fiscal year,' declared the *Bangkok Post* in January 1960. 'Thailand with its 24 million population is getting 23 million US dollars while it is reported that Cambodia with four to five million population is getting 20 million dollars and Laos with two to three million population is getting 120 million dollars. . . . Does the United States value so little Thailand's firm stand with the Free World? Has Thailand's strategic position in South-East Asia apparently so little significance in the US concept of defence of democracy, American interests and the American way of life? . . .'

Aid to neutrals, of course, is part of a world-wide policy which may well be hard to understand from a local viewpoint. Particularly disturbing to Thailand was America's decision of May 1960 to supply India with sixteen million tons of surplus wheat and one million tons of rice over the next four years. 'We want to cheer the deal,' said Thanat Khoman, Foreign Minister, 'but when we think of the fifteen million or so farmers of Thailand who are suffering from the consequences of low paddy prices, the cheers choke in our throats.' The mere possibility of the sale of surplus American rice to Singapore creates equal concern over interference with Thai markets. 'What advantages are there for Thailand to remain in Free World ties,' well-informed sources enquire, 'when countries not at all committed to the Free World are getting at least equal benefits and, in addition to these, advantages of Communist aid?'

The situation in Laos provides another example. From the day of Captain Kong Lae's *coup* in August 1960, official

---

* American military aid for 1962, however, amounted to over $58 million. The US has over 200 military advisers working with the Thai armed forces, which number about 100,000, mostly in the Army. Thailand has been supplied with light tanks, howitzers, rifles and machine guns, trucks, transport planes and jet fighters.

reaction in Thailand was bitterly and determinedly hostile. No trade was allowed between Thailand and Vientiane, ostensibly because of unstable conditions and to protect the safety of Thai merchants; yet almost all the imports of Laos have to come by rail from Bangkok, including rice and petrol. The *coup* leaders were then said to be collaborating openly with the Pathet Lao. Prince Souphanouvong himself was living in the house with his half-brother, Prince Souvanna Phouma, according to Thai Government reports. 'The open support of Communist propaganda,' declared Radio Thailand on August 27th, 'may be interpreted as meaning that everything that has happened in Laos happened in accordance with Communist plans.'

Fear of Communism blinded the Government to the realities of the situation. Yet the Prime Minister admitted by October 1960 that foreign governments: 'One, do not believe the Thai evaluation of the facts of events in Laos. Two, do not believe that Prince Souvanna Phouma is pro-Communist. Three, charge that Thailand, which has only announced an anti-Communist policy, is interfering in Laos. Four, believe Prince Souvanna Phouma's charges that Thailand has closed the border and is applying economic pressure on Laos.' In obvious pique against America's reluctance to back Thailand fully over Laos, the Prime Minister suddenly started negotiations for 'economic co-operation' with Russia. Yet one of his arguments for condemning the Souvanna Phouma regime was the latter's acceptance of Soviet aid.

Thailand's attitude, however, is understandable. The situation in Laos affects her more closely than it does any other country. And what could be more natural than to support a right-wing general, whose views coincide with those of Bangkok, rather than a neutralist politician, half-brother of the rebel leader himself? The mistake, and of course it was shared by others, was to overestimate the appeal of General Phoumi and the strength of his army. Yet the very fact of the revolt by Kong Lae and his revelations of corruption should have dispelled any illusions on this score: Laos is a country not so much divided against itself as divided into many pieces, held together more in theory than in practice. No amount of military support to an unpopular and incapable regime could guarantee either the pacification or unity of the country. And even were the country to go Communist, which is possible, is this quite the menace to Thailand that it seems?

Thai leaders now accept 'a genuinely neutral Laos', provided it does not become Communist. What they fear is a 'Czechoslovakia Deal', i.e. the legalized surrender of occupied areas to the Pathet Lao, and still more a 'Czechoslovak *coup*', placing the entire country behind the Iron Curtain. But what were the effects of the Communist *coup* in Prague? The shock and revulsion felt by the West more than anything else brought the rest of Europe into a solidarity of alliance against Russia. The well-aired view that once a piece of territory goes—say Quemoy or Laos—all the rest goes too, is totally lacking in all sense of proportion. It may affect prestige—hardly that in these two cases (though South Vietnam and even Taiwan are quite a different matter)—but it should never affect national determination to survive.

Varying interpretations of the situation in Laos, and hence what to do about it, have however brought severe strains on the alliance of which Thailand is the key member—the South-East Asia Treaty Organization. SEATO has long proclaimed that it is a protective shield for the whole 'Treaty Area'. Since SEATO was formed, it declares, no Communist aggression has occurred in South-East Asia. Meanwhile Laos is endangered. What should SEATO do? Instead of marching to the battle-front, SEATO sits down and talks: such is the Thai reaction. Of course the Organization was never intended to be a mobile police force—it has no joint command, or even armed forces, of its own—to put down subversion and infiltration here and there. Aggression is one thing, subversion, even civil war, quite another. SEATO in fact has limited objectives and dealing with an essentially political situation—or what should be political—is not one of them.

However, the frustration of the Thai leaders over Laos is evident, for, according to Marshal Sarit, appointment of Prince Souvanna Phouma as Prime Minister would be a 'sign of victory for the Communists'; and this reflects on their attitude to SEATO. The 'enemy', the Marshal pointed out in an address on SEATO Day (September 8, 1961), charges SEATO with intervening in Laos; its friends, with 'failing to act in any way that would save Laos from the Communist danger'. It was therefore 'high time' to 'reform' the organization, because the 'interests of some member countries do not correspond with those of the majority'. The Prime Minister told reporters that he 'would like' decisions by a majority and not—as at present—by the unanimous vote of all members; two member countries— France and Britain—'never agreed with the majority', which 'prevented any action' over Laos. The Thai Foreign Minister proposed that 'the people of Thailand' should decide whether to withdraw from SEATO if the Prime Minister's reforms were not carried out; but the 'people' had not decided anything for some time, observed a Thai correspondent. In fact, in whatever manner decisions were reached, the disadvantages of a forward policy in Laos would remain: troops bogged down in a terrain suitable chiefly for guerrillas; and the likelihood of Chinese intervention.

US policy has also come under fire. Washington's insistence on a coalition government in Laos to include the Pathet Lao and withholding aid to Vientiane would, according to the Thai Minister of Defence on January 11, 1962, 'expedite the Communist takeover of Laos'. The Prime Minister added that if anything happened 'suddenly' in Laos, he might have to use 'central funds to meet the emergency'. Thai troops, in mid-February, were sent to man the northern frontier, near Nam Tha. Not long afterwards the Thai Government was greatly reassured by the joint statement signed by Thanat Khoman and Dean Rusk in Washington (March 6, 1962). Both agreed that SEATO 'provides the basis' for collective assistance to Thailand 'in case of Communist armed attack'. The US 'intends to give full effect to its obligations under the (SEATO) treaty', but this 'does not depend upon the prior agreement of all other parties . . . since this treaty obligation is individual as well as collective'. As for 'indirect aggression', US economic and military assistance provide 'an important basis for US action to help Thailand'.

This gave Thailand more confidence in SEATO, commented Thanat, and there was less urgency for reforms such as granting wider powers to the Secretary-General. The joint statement also smoothed the way for a more constructive Thai policy on Laos—though newspaper attacks on Souvanna

Phouma and Western statesmen were allowed to continue, notably in *Sarn Seri*, which is considered the mouthpiece of the Field Marshal. It became known by the end of March that Thailand was willing to see a government headed by Prince Souvanna Phouma tried out in Laos provided the coalition government were genuinely neutral and remained so. But despite Averell Harriman's remark in Bangkok that 'Souvanna is not dominated by the Communists' and that Marshal Sarit was 'in entire agreement' with the US position, the Thai Government maintained its opposition to any 'coercion' of Vientiane and still believed the neutralist leader was 'more or less' under Communist control.*

For all that, Thailand is far and away the chief beneficiary from the existence of SEATO. Her frontiers are guaranteed against attack; but problems of subversion are, as they must be, her own affair. (It is only policy than can cure the *causes* of subversion, neither police forces nor an armed alliance.) And by its very inactivity over Laos, SEATO has demonstrated to the uncommitted nations that it is neither reckless nor aggressive. With the power of China looming so large, there is a place for collective defence in the area.

---

* Eleven days after Nam Tha fell to the Pathet Lao (May 6, 1962) US troops landed in Thailand. Almost half of them—nearly 3,000 Marines—were withdrawn following the Geneva Agreement on Laos. Thai 'responsible circles' voiced fears (*Bankok Post*, July 24, 1962) that if the West 'forsook' Thailand, a policy of neutrality might be indicated; the alternative was not assistance by the 'impotent' SEATO, but a 'bilateral mutual defence agreement with the United States'.

CHAPTER 7

OVERSEAS CHINESE

Starting on a certain day in February or March, practically all the shops and most of the businesses in Bangkok, Kuala Lumpur, Singapore and Saigon close down. Many shops shut—usually for three days or more—in Rangoon, Phnom Penh, Manila and even Jakarta. Virtually the whole of South-East Asia suffers a partial or complete economic eclipse. This is not a conspiracy; it is the Chinese New Year.

It is also almost the only occasion on which the overseas Chinese demonstrate their power. For the rest of the year (with minor exceptions) the Chinese are hard at work, shops and factories open often late at night and every day of the week. Their attitude to the countries they live in is expressed in the saying: 'We don't mind who holds the head of the cow, provided we can milk it.' But this shrewd refusal to meddle in politics cannot altogether allay the natural fears of the indigenous population. It was King Vajiravud of Thailand who denounced the 'Jews of the East' and echoed the European warnings of the time against the 'yellow peril'.

This is not, after all, so surprising. Imagine (with a change of scene) the City of London entirely run by Russians, except for some struggling British firms largely dependent on Russian advice, and even capital, as well as one or two big American enterprises. Imagine Paris, Rome and Berlin in the same position: and a country like Italy with half its population Russians, proudly observing their own customs and language, separate and distinct from the Italians. Above all, a hostile Russian continent looms beyond the frail frontiers of these deeply-penetrated Western nations.

This is a fair picture of the situation in South-East Asia. More than half the inhabitants of Bangkok, for example, are Chinese (though many have Thai nationality). Nearly one in seven of the total population of Thailand is Chinese, almost

50 per cent in Malaya, about a tenth in South Vietnam and more than eight out of every ten in Singapore. In absolute terms, there are some three million 'ethnic' Chinese (aliens and those nationals whose speech and customs are Chinese) in Thailand; nearly three million in Malaya and two million in Indonesia; a million in Singapore and in South Vietnam; and over a million altogether in Burma, Borneo, Cambodia and the Philippines.

PRIVATE ENTERPRISE

The countries of South-East Asia grow rice (for subsistence or export), and also cultivate rubber, coffee, coconut and teak, and extract tin and oil. While the peasants produce the crops, it is the Chinese who buy them up, transport, store and market them. The Chinese lend money, open trading stores in villages, carry their goods on shoulder poles, in carts or boats throughout the land. Poor Chinese work at the docks, in small workshops, factories, rice and saw-mills. Middling Chinese sit in shops and offices and size up their customers with a shrewdness and awareness very different from the open nature of the local population. Wealthy Chinese build hotels, found banks, set up huge export/import concerns. In some countries they still live inconspicuously, not flaunting their wealth for fear of political consequences—and the tax collector; in others, they reside in air-conditioned villas or red-pillared mansions, often surrounded by barbed-wire fences and protected by dogs for fear of thieves and kidnappers.

The overseas Chinese have the true pioneering spirit. Arriving (or at least their grandfathers arriving) with almost nothing in a strange land, by their own industry, patience and self-sacrifice they have made their way. 'You are now working abroad,' Richard L. Walker quotes a wife in China writing to her husband overseas (in his *Letters from the Communes*). 'You must fight to get ahead. A man creates his own future. Money is for those who fight for it. . . . You are an overseas Chinese. If you do not succeed, people sneer at us at home, and say "unsuccessful". . . . Husband, determine and struggle on. You will be able to overcome all difficulties.'

This is the same spirit of enterprise shown by all settlers or colonizers. And it has provoked similar controversies. Do the overseas Chinese develop an economy which otherwise would remain poor and primitive, as they claim, or do they rather exploit a country's resources, produce nothing themselves but live off the labour of others, as their critics say? President Sukarno's ban on 'alien' retail traders in Indonesian villages is explained to a large extent by the real, or imagined, grievances felt by the Indonesians. In Thailand, on the other hand, there may be grumbling or envy at the success of the Chinese in a field in which South-East Asians hardly compete, but they are generally accepted without resentment. The answer to the question of development or exploitation lies, as usual in such cases, somewhere between the extremes.

Put moderately, as by a former Mayor of Rangoon, 'it is an undeniable fact that the Chinese have played an important part in the economy of the country, but if a few Chinese nationals dabble in its internal affairs there is a possibility that Sino-Burmese friendship may suffer'. And less moderately from the other side, admittedly in protest against the Indonesian ban: 'In the old China days, overseas Chinese were helpless. . . . If there are still some people who imagine that the Chinese Government and the 650 million Chinese will remain unmoved at the unreasonable discrimination against and persecution of overseas Chinese, they are committing a gross error.' Divided as they are by economic status and origin (Hokkiens, Cantonese, Hakkas, Teochius and Hainanese speak different 'dialects' and form separate clubs or associations), most overseas Chinese still regard China, under any form of Government, as their protector. The difference is that the Nationalists were too harassed or preoccupied to do very much for their compatriots (it was rather the other way round), whereas the Communists have drastically reasserted Chinese power and prestige. Figures vary as to the ratio of 'pro-Peking' to 'pro-Taiwan' overseas Chinese. But it may be taken as roughly two to one—regardless of the local government's opinion—with the gap widening as the mainland sponsors a peace offensive (as at Bandung), or lessening as it fails in agriculture or launches the communes.

Pride in China and the need for reinsurance in the future, rather than ideology, determines their attitude. (Such exponents of private enterprise as the overseas Chinese could hardly settle for collectivization.) But it is still an attitude alien to the original inhabitants of the countries where they have settled. Ultimately the solution, if South-East Asia is to remain independent, must be assimilation. Restrictions, for example on teaching Chinese, certainly provide pressure to conform. So, more effectively, does intermarriage (though religion, in Moslem countries, is a barrier). But whatever the difficulties, the Chinese need to feel that they belong.

RESTRICTIONS

The industrious Chinese are not always easy for the local inhabitants to accept. 'What is of the utmost importance,' stated *Siam Rath* a few years ago, 'is that in the Bangkok of today Chinese are to be found everywhere in the city. . . . They are becoming more and more numerous daily, pushing Thais out of the city steadily in order to make more room for themselves. . . . Should Bangkok fall entirely into the hands of Chinese it would be a most serious danger threatening independence, freedom and security.' The newspaper advocated that Chinese should be restricted to a specified area called 'Chinatown'.

In 1958 a special committee headed by the then Prime Minister, General Thanom, listed three 'dangers to the nation'—political parties in violent opposition to Government policies, public opinion similarly opposed, and 'aliens and minorities . . . subverting the nation politically and economically'.

'It is generally known,' the committee observed, 'that economic power has fallen into alien hands. Foreigners do not feel any love for this country. It is necessary to take measures to keep watch on these aliens.' Aliens injuring Thai people intentionally or acting in mobs against law and order will be liable to deportation, stated the Ministry of the Interior (also in 1958) and so will 'aliens who cause economic disturbances through manipulations of foreign exchange, profiteering and malpractices in trade'.

The present Prime Minister, Marshal Sarit, received a proposal in July 1960 for a 'three-stage programme for Thai take-over of the commerce of Thailand from aliens', but officials considered it too drastic. The first stage was for commercial houses to employ only Thais—at present, firms are required to have 75 per cent of them. At the end of the second stage all retail shops and small businesses should belong to Thais; and by the third, all commerce would be taken over. Police and interior officials directly concerned with the problem, however, thought the Chinese in Thailand were a lesser danger than they were in neighbouring countries. Chinese children educated in the higher schools do not like to behave like Chinese, the officials reported, but like to consider themselves Thai.* 'However, it is difficult to know how they actually feel in their hearts.' They suggested that the Chinese should receive fairer treatment, and not be mistreated: 'this would be beneficial to the country'. Nothing too drastic should be done, but at the same time 'we cannot be too careful'. Police stations throughout the country were even instructed, in October 1961, to assume a 'friendly and mild attitude' towards Chinese contacting the authorities on official business—even if they could not speak Thai fluently. The Minister of the Interior pointed out that the bulk of Chinese in Thailand were law-abiding and had contributed greatly to the country.

In general, despite press entreaties, this sensible policy is followed. At least the problem gets no bigger, for the annual quota of Chinese allowed to enter the country is restricted to 200 only. (Before the war up to 100,000 entered a year, though a large proportion went back again too; the present quota was imposed in 1949.) From 1961, every immigrant must also deposit—or invest—the sum of 100,000 baht (nearly £1,700 or $5,000) as a guarantee of financial security. The cost of a residence permit stands at 1,000 baht, and there is a yearly poll-tax to pay.

There is an extensive and varied Chinese middle class, Skinner reports in his pioneering work, *Chinese Society in Thailand*. Nearly two-thirds of the Chinese are Teochius

* In Bangkok, about half the students in universities and high schools are *lukjin* (children of Chinese parents) who study Thai during the day and Chinese at night. However, 'when they have completed their education,' reported the Thai Minister of Education in August 1961, 'they, having come from business families, return to trade and they co-operate with Chinese circles, declining to co-operate with the Thai Government. . . .'

(originally from Swatow); they are predominantly mill-owners, revenue farmers, pawnbrokers, dockers and labourers. Cantonese (7 per cent) are engineers, mechanics and construction workers, also hotel and restaurant-owners. Hakkas (16 per cent) are petty traders; and Hainanese (11 per cent) are servants, waiters and coolies, the poorest of them all. Most of the rubber exporters are Hokkiens (4 per cent), who are the chief Chinese community in Malaya; almost all rice merchants are Teochius. The father of Pridi, Skinner states, was a Teochiu and so was the father of another Prime Minister, Phya Bahon.

The Teochiu Association, largest of the Chinese Societies in Bangkok, was under the control of Peking sympathizers for six years up to 1960. (In Thailand, 60 per cent of the overseas Chinese support Peking, 30 per cent Taiwan, and 10 per cent 'don't know'.) The Association owns two big Chinese schools and a cemetery. Other associations run schools and hospitals— the Chinese have a great respect for education and a long tradition of community welfare.

From time to time Communist activities are reported among the Chinese. Two Hakka Communist terrorists from Malaya were arrested in November 1960 only twenty days after one of them had started work in Bangkok as a tailor (90 per cent of Chinese tailors are Hakkas). Thirteen staff members of a Chinese school in South Thailand, including the headmaster, were arrested three months before in a police round-up of Communist suspects and nearly seven hundred pupils were left without teachers. Altogether some 270 Chinese Communists are being held at Lard Yao Gaol, Bangkok.

A large quantity of mainland Chinese goods, mostly pickled foodstuffs and dried fruits, was seized from a Chinese grocery store in December 1960. These dangerous substances, and all other goods from China, have been banned since January 1959. The ban came at the tail-end of a Chinese trade offensive which spread alarm and despondency throughout South-East Asia—and throughout the ranks of Japanese and Indian competitors. The actual value of goods from China entering Thailand was only about 5 per cent of total imports in 1958, but certain items had increased sharply. Examples are newsprint, textiles (sarongs, poplins, towels and table-cloths), iron and steel bars, plates and wire, nuts and bolts, and most types of office equipment. Terms of trade were generous, the Bank of China extending credit to local banks. Merchants who had suffered losses on one shipment of Chinese goods were reported to have been granted sufficiently reduced prices on the next to recover their losses. Pricing of textiles was flexible: China seemed intent on capturing the low-grade textile market regardless of how much prices had to be reduced.

Despite the argument of some Thai officials that cheap Chinese goods helped keep down the cost of living, the Government decided on a total ban.* On the last day that sales were permitted, one shop in Bangkok was said to have sold two thousand watches at a 40 per cent discount. Thermos flasks went for even less. Prices of canned foods, stationery, china, glassware and medicines were slashed. Elsewhere the Chinese trade offensive, watched with such gloomy alarm, just petered out. It was all due to a miscalculation by Peking. China at that time desperately needed foreign exchange and so started a big sales campaign among the overseas Chinese. Unfortunately it was a falling market and China had to sell her goods more cheaply than she had intended. But the more she sold—to gain the needed exchange—the more the prices fell.

Trade in the reverse direction is also banned. But remittances to China continue. Chinese residents in Thailand who used to remit seventy million baht (well over £1 million or $3½ million) a year now send home only a fraction of that sum; the amount fell from forty-four million baht in 1958 to only eleven million in 1959, according to the Bank of Thailand. Many overseas Chinese believed their savings were not going to their relatives in China but to the communes instead.

PARTNERSHIP

A noted Chinese trader, millionaire owner of a chain of hotels and nightclubs, Wu Yung-ken (Chit Kitpanit is his Thai name), was arrested in 1960 on a charge of smuggling fish from Cambodia into Thailand. After months of legal enquiries, Wu was

---

* Imports from China were considered a threat to security since funds from the sale of these goods were believed to have been used to finance Communist activities in Thailand.

deported to Taiwan. To avoid similar difficulties, most influential Chinese have long since gone into partnership with the Thai authorities. A Hakka Chinese leader managing the Thai Development Bank in 1960 invited a Thai general, deputy-commander of the First Army, to become Chairman of the Board. In 1959, twelve Chinese transport companies formed a syndicate and asked one police general and six police colonels to join the Board of Directors. The Chinese business community regularly donate sums for Thai public works. The late Chairman of the Chinese Chamber of Commerce, Chang Lan-chen, outbid all others at a recent charity auction to buy a portrait of the King and Queen. Speaking in September 1961 to officers of Chinese guilds and associations, the acting Chairman gave this characteristic advice: 'We Chinese merchants should unite and strengthen our co-operation in furthering the economic policy of the Government on the one hand and promoting our personal business on the other.'

This 'system' of co-operation, as Skinner calls it, started in the reigns of King Mongkut and King Chulalongkorn, both of whom encouraged leading Chinese to enter Thai service. Their policy was to 'ennoble every Chinese important because of riches or influence', Skinner cites a contemporary writer, Bastian, 'and thus draw him into the interests of the country . . . Chinese of wealth often become favourites with the rulers and receive titles of nobility and these noblemen in return present their daughters to their majesties'. Their descendants are among the leading Thai families; some are in business, many in Government.

The turning point came in 1910, Skinner writes, with the death of Chulalongkorn. The new king, Vajiravud, was a fervent Thai nationalist. The Chinese called a general strike against the yearly poll tax, but this was a disastrous failure. Thai leaders, after 1932, intensified the nationalistic policy. In 1939, shop signs were taxed, but the tax was increased tenfold if more than half the sign was not written in Thai; regulations provided for a 75 per cent Thai labour force. Various occupations were reserved for Thais (including of course, Thai nationals of Chinese origin, otherwise the system would have broken down). The post-war Government sought greater participation in business. A large number of semi-official agencies were created, such as the Express Transport Organization, the Thai Financial Syndicate, the War Veterans Organization, and so on. Thai agencies lacked the experience and acumen of the Chinese; the latter, faced with endless official forms and restrictions, lacked the necessary contacts with Thai authority. It was only a question of time before they came together. The desire for profits on the one hand and security on the other, Skinner relates, forced the alliance between Thai nationalists and Chinese merchants. The Thai élite joined boards of directors of Chinese firms—two-thirds of the big insurance companies, eight out of the ten major non-Western banks or trusts and two-thirds of the export-import and shipping firms. The irony of the situation, Skinner observes, is that 'militant economic nationalism has resulted, not in the defeat of the enemy, but in co-operation between the antagonists'.

CHAPTER 8

ECONOMIC CHANGE

⟶❀❁❧

Thailand is the size of France, with just over half the population. The average yearly income per head is some 2,000 baht (£34 or $100), about nine times below that of France, but 40 per cent more than in India. As in most of Asia, nine out of ten Thais live in villages and one in towns. Of the working population, seven out of ten cultivate rice.

AGRICULTURE

Half Thailand's rice is produced in the Central Plain (93 per cent is white rice). The North-East, with the same amount of land under rice, produces under a third (three-quarters of it is glutinous, or 'sticky', rice). The Central Plain has the biggest surplus for export and the most rice mills (usually owned by Chinese). Though the area under rice—over fourteen million acres—has increased slightly in the last ten years, the yield has remained the same. It has actually declined, by almost one-third, in comparison with the 1923–27 harvest.*

Rice for years has been Thailand's biggest export earner. In 1960 for the first time it was equalled by rubber, grown in the South. The production of rubber increased from 115,000 metric tons in 1950 to 174,000 tons nine years later. Rubber and rice were each about one-third in value of total exports in 1960. But while earnings from rice went up over the previous year by only five million baht (on an export total of 8,569 million baht, over £140 million or $425 million) rubber went up by 243 million, tin by 107 million, teak by 112, maize 300 (doubling)

---

* The present yield (1954–58) is 440 lb. per *rai* (⅖ acre). The average yield by regions in 1956 was: Central Plain 1,408 lb. per acre; North-East 990, North 1,903; and South 1,353. In 1960 the total area under rice was 14½ million acres; production was 7.46 million tons.

and jute 141 million (two and a half times). The situation has altered in 1961; rice sales are up, rubber down (despite higher output), kenaf (with jute) and tapioca flour greatly increased, tin has improved and maize is about the same.

CHIEF EXPORTS
(million baht)

	1957	1960
Rice	3,943	2,582
Rubber	1,689	2,579
Tin	531	536
Teak	262	357
Tapioca	138	267
Tobacco	100	n.a.
Castor beans	87	71
Maize (corn)	74	551
Live cattle	58	100 (with pigs)
Kenaf/jute	—	230

(Source: Bank of Thailand)

Rice farming, the basic occupation, is no longer making progress. Tin and rubber, produced by relatively few workers in the South, are now major sources of foreign exchange. Secondary crops, like maize, cotton, tobacco and jute, are making spectacular increases. These are crops suited to the uplands of the North-East, crops which can redeem that distressed area and, at the same time, lessen the country's dependence on rice.

A report on a 'self-help settlement' near Bangkok illustrates these possibilities. The settlement is at Saraburi, about eighty miles by road north of Bangkok. A farm wife told Theh Chongkhadikij (*Bangkok Post*, August 6, 1959):

'My husband decided to give up *samlor* driving three years ago. We came here to try farming. We were given 25 *rai* (ten acres) of virgin land. We spent the first two years in clearing the land and breaking it in and last year we got a corn (maize) crop that brought us an income of 20,000 baht (£330, $1,000). . . . It is about the same (as a *samlor*-driver's income). But what was earned as a Bangkok *samlor* driver we could not keep. We had to spend as much and as fast as we earned. . . . (Now) in another two years we will be entitled to a title-deed.

We will have land for our children to inherit and develop.'

Some of the obstacles facing the early farmers were described by a widow who went to the settlement with her seven children and a sum of 500 baht (under £9 or $25) in 1941. The place, she said, was mainly a jungle with elephants and other wild animals. Malaria killed a number of families in those early days. But she cleared the land, grew maize, planted bananas, jackfruit and mango trees and made charcoal from timber. Now she has 50 *rai* of land, four lorries for carrying her produce to market and a general goods store. She earns 50 to 60,000 baht (up to £100, or nearly $300) a year.

A former rice farmer from Lopburi told this reporter that he was now earning far more from rotation crops like maize, cotton and peanuts. 'You plant rice only once a year. . . . With a 50 *rai* rice farm I would get only 10,000 baht a year. I have only 25 *rai* here but I am getting 20,000 baht income.'

The settlement is carefully planned with a main road twenty-five miles long and a total of 100 miles of side roads. These 'feeder' roads are essential for bringing farm produce to market. Roads are passable throughout the year, but with some difficulty in the rains. The settlers, 12,000 families in all, have bought buses and started services to Saraburi and Bangkok. They have built three *wats* (monasteries) and three schools. The settled area, over 100,000 acres, is now almost free from malaria; there is a DDT drive every year. Water is the chief problem, but two artesian wells and two irrigation tanks have been dug and two more are planned. Electricity is within half a dozen miles of the settlement, bought from Phra Buddhabat town—site of the 'Buddha's Footprint', a famous place of pilgrimage for both Thais and Chinese. Seven tractors are hired by the Government to settlers at the rate of about forty-five shillings (seven dollars) an acre. Settlers sell their produce through co-operative marketing societies.

This is an example of what can happen with proper land surveys, access roads, water supplies, malaria control and police protection—and reliance, as the International Bank mission puts it, on 'natural development', that is, the initiative of the Thai farmers themselves. Better technical services are wanted rather than extensive programmes of community development, the mission considers in its valuable report, *A*

Public Development Program for Thailand. Unlike such countries as India or Pakistan there is no serious rural indebtedness. Nearly all farmers own their land and they are independent and resourceful. 'They feel unoppressed and free, there are no subservient castes, and each village has the stabilizing and sometimes stimulating influence of its Buddhist temple.' The villagers are lively and intelligent enough, the mission believes, to accept change if they see value in it.

Technical services, however, are 'sadly deficient', the mission observes. 'The farmer does not lack initiative, but his ambitions are modest and his knowledge is limited to the traditional.' Research is specially needed on upland farming, the yield and quantity of rice, and resistance to pests and diseases. Rice and crops could be doubled by means of an assured and regular water supply, proper care of the nursery bed (for the rice seedlings before transplanting), good levelling and bunding of fields, ploughing and harrowing for weed control, and proper spacing of plants. Good seed selection alone could raise yields by up to one-fifth. Fertilizer, which is very little used,* could bring about a remarkable increase: it is the basis of Japanese rice cultivation, a model for the Far East.

Traditional ways are no longer enough—such is the burden of the International Bank's penetrating report. More effective action is needed if the momentum of the economy and the welfare of a growing population—which has doubled in thirty years—is to be maintained. Thailand's economy is critically dependent on a few basic products—rice, rubber, tin and teak. Over a million tons of rice are exported every year (out of a total crop of seven to eight million tons) but the market is becoming more and more competitive. Burma exports a million and a half tons; before the war it was about three million. Cambodia and South Vietnam are also rice exporters. China, before recent failures, has exported—mostly to the Soviet Union—over a million tons a year. Of the importing countries, Japan is now almost self-sufficient in rice, and Malaya and Pakistan are working towards this goal. Indonesia, however, with its severe internal problems, and India and

* Imported fertilizer costs the Thai farmer three baht (one shilling or 15 cents) a kilogram; it should sell at a quarter of that price when a fertilizer plant is built in the North.

K

Ceylon, are still large importers. None of these traditional markets can be taken for granted. Even if the Thai surplus can be raised beyond the needs of an expanding population (now 27 million) there is no guaranteed outlet for the future.

Tin—which can be discussed here for convenience—faces a similar problem of demand. A strict quota, imposed by the International Tin Commission, reduced Thai production from 18,600 tons in 1957 to only 10,000 tons a year later. World demand at that time was only three-quarters of productive capacity, which was about 180,000 tons. Since then consumption has steadily risen and it is now a question of Malaya (the largest producer), Indonesia, Bolivia, Thailand and the Congo producing enough to meet it.*

Rubber faces increasing competition from the synthetic product. Yet demand for natural rubber is high and producers in Malaya, Thailand and Indonesia are fairly optimistic. Teak, on the contrary, has been drastically over-sold—often by illegal traders—and the virtual extinction of the industry is threatened unless replanting is carried out and forest protection enforced.†

Thailand can develop most products considerably, the mission reports. Much of the Central Plain could produce two or more crops of rice a year if enough water could be stored and distributed when needed to the fields. Farmers have little to do but sit through the hot, dry weather of March and April, waiting for the first rains of May to prepare their fields for planting. Even in the six-month cycle of June to December, when the seedlings are laboriously transplanted by hand (from the nursery bed to the open, flooded fields), to the time of harvesting and threshing at the end of the year, there are long periods of enforced, if not unwelcome, idleness.

Irrigation is essential in Thailand, as Ingram has pointed out in *Economic Change in Thailand since 1850*. There is insufficient

---

* Leading producers (thousand metric tons per month) of tin: Malaya 4·40; Indonesia 1·9; Bolivia 1·6; Thailand 1·02; Congo 0·85; and of rubber: Malaya 60·2; Indonesia 50·4; Thailand 14·2; Ceylon 8·2; South Vietnam 6·5 (1960 figures). By 1961 world consumption of synthetic rubber nearly equalled that of natural; consumption of synthetic had grown over three-fold between 1949 and 1959, that of natural rubber only by half.

† Two prominent timber merchants of North Thailand and four forest officials were charged in July 1961 with illegally felling two thousand teak trees valued at six million baht.

rainfall for rice—seventy inches are needed without irrigation—and the river supply is unreliable. Taken over the past hundred years, only one year in three has a 'good' water supply, one year is average, and one year crops are damaged considerably. As far back as 1903, a Dutch irrigation expert, Van der Heide, proposed to construct an irrigation dam at Chainat. The plan, costing 47 million baht, would take twelve years to complete, but it was rejected on financial grounds. Yet the crop failure of 1919-20 alone, Ingram states, cost the nation more than the entire cost of the works planned. Nearly fifty years later, only four million *rai*—out of thirty-six million *rai* under rice—were irrigated. Even now, with the construction of the Chainat dam (in 1956) and twice the area of irrigated land, only two million *rai* receive an assured and adequate supply of water at the right time every year.

Rubber potential is equally large—and equally neglected, the International Bank reports. Twice the land now being cultivated in the South is suitable for rubber, or three times if terraces are used. Even within the present area, output could be tripled by proper management and by replanting with high-yielding trees. Two and a half million *rai* are planted under rubber and at least one million of them need replanting, as the trees are thirty to fifty years old. Most of the owners are small-holders who need assistance; they own about two million *rai*, and are chiefly Thais, though a good number are Chinese by origin; the large owners are Chinese. A 'cess act' was passed in 1960 to provide funds for replanting (as in Malaya), for it takes six or seven years before the new trees are mature. Thai rubber costs over seven baht a kilo to produce, while in Malaya—where 60 per cent of it is grown on plantations—it is about five baht. But, *rai* for *rai*, rubber is twice as profitable to cultivate in Thailand as rice.

Upland crops are almost more profitable, according to Niwat Tulyayon (in the *Far Eastern Economic Review* of January 4th and March 22, 1962). The average gross income from an acre of maize (corn) is about 750 baht, while that of rice is only 450. Besides, maize can be grown twice a year, though fertilizer is always required. A grower of kenaf (a fibre crop similar to jute, but extensively cultivated in the Centre and North-East) also earns 750 baht an acre, while his costs of production—

labour, seeds and transport—and rent charges amount to 500 baht. Japan is the largest market for Thailand's kenaf and maize. The International Bank mission believes in rain-fed cultivation in the North-East, replacing the traditional reliance on rice. River irrigation is difficult—one of the reasons for the neglect of the North-East—because of irregular flooding, rapid run-off and loss of water through seepage into the ground. Erosion in the North and North-East is particularly serious as a result of the primitive but widely practised habit of shifting cultivation. About a million peasants live by 'slash and burn' farming—cutting down the forests, burning the timber, planting the rice for two or three seasons and then moving on. Not only does this exhaust the soil, but it has the worst possible effects on the water supply. The natural storage of water disappears when the forests are cut down, and there is nothing to hold the water back during the rains. The result is destructive floods in one season, drought in the other.

The people of the North-East, according to a United Nations expert, Dr Thieme, need assistance in changing over from rice farming to oil seeds, jute and cotton, castor seeds, sesame and ground nuts. Fertilizer plants should be set up to use vegetable waste, and roads, for marketing produce, should be improved. An Australian Colombo Plan adviser toured the North-East in September 1961 to report on the construction of feeder roads. 'In the villages out from Khonkaen and other cities further north,' he noted, 'there are people living in productive areas who are ready to assist the nation's economy with crops of jute, maize and rice, but who must cart it over tedious distances which in bad weather defy even the most hardy bullock carts. . . . Their marketable output is consequently small and their life is restricted.'

The present Government is indeed making considerable efforts to develop the region. The Prime Minister is chairman of the committee on development of the North-East, which is to spend 6,000 million baht in its five year plan, starting in 1962; and the Finance Minister has been surveying possibilities both there and in the South. Japan, too, is prepared to co-operate, according to an agreement reached in November 1961, in establishing a Technical Training Centre in the North-East (as well as to repay the full outstanding amount of 570 million baht remaining from a war-time 'loan'). But centuries of poverty do not make for modern initiative: 'Without much hope of extracting from the earth more than a bare subsistence,' writes Theh Chongkhadikij, 'the people (of the North-East) do not take matters too seriously. . . . They discard work at any stage, not caring whether the moment of leaving is critical to the success or failure of the job, in order to walk many kilometres to a fair. . . . Their status symbols are different from those of the Western world. To them, according to the *phuyaiban* (headman of a village), it is the grandeur of a ceremony of a son's entry into temporary monkhood or of a house-warming or of a cremating party that counts. . . . So debts are incurred for non-productive spending. And who profits? The usurers with their high interest rates who tie up a farmer's crop in advance for repayment in kind. They force the farmers to price their crop low and they sell with a wide margin to the processors. . . .'*

Besides these special celebrations, something like 10 per cent of each family's income is spent on the upkeep of the village monastery or on religious gifts, and rice is handed over every day to the monks.

Into this traditional society springs the new plan for economic development. Agricultural production throughout Thailand is scheduled to increase by 3 per cent a year under the first Six Year Plan, which started in October 1961; yearly percentage rates for certain products are given as:

Rice	1/3	Teak	5	Maize	50
Rubber	6	Tapioca	7	Livestock	3

Fish Catches   8: at present about 200,000 tons a year are caught; after Japan, Thailand is the biggest exporter of fish in Asia.

* Only one fifth of farm families reported some indebtedness, according to a survey in 1953, but the study of a typical village in Thailand, states the *Bangkok Bank Monthly Review* (January 1961), reveals a rate of interest charged from 10 to 67 per cent a season. The rate of long-term loans was 2 per cent a month. Money-lenders and landlords charged the highest rates, 30 and 44 per cent respectively. Friends and relatives charged over 18 per cent, co-operatives only 8½ per cent. There are two reasons for these high rates. The first is that loans are subject to high risks, chiefly from natural disasters, and hence the rate of default is high. Secondly, little or no collateral is offered, which makes the lender think twice before he parts with his money. (Government has set aside 10 million baht for the agricultural credit programme for 1961, but 4,000 million baht are needed for a long-term programme, states the Minister of Finance.)

Forests are to be reserved and protected until they cover half the country.

These objectives are to be achieved:

(1) Through irrigation, with priority to the Chao Phya and Yanhee projects (see below).

(2) By improved production methods, through pilot farms, propagating techniques, diversification of crops, rotation farming, improved quality, use of fertilizer and action against pests.

(3) By village development, especially in the North-East.

(4) By land surveys and classification of the soil.

(5) By improving self-help settlements and establishing settlements for the hill tribes.

(6) By encouragement of co-operative societies—members at present number some 400,000—which are to become self-supporting.

BASIC SERVICES

Rather than Government setting up its own industries, Ingram wrote in 1955, it would be far better for it to develop the basic public services by means of which private industry and agriculture could prosper. The International Bank mission also advised, in 1959, that there should be no further Government ventures in industry. Private enterprise, it said, should be encouraged by tax inducements, credit concessions and so forth.

Irrigation, agricultural research, transport and communications, provision of electric power and better education—these are some of the basic services the experts recommend. Government aid to development—long held back by a conservative financial policy*—has greatly increased since the end of the

* For nearly a hundred years, Ingram asserts, safeguarding the international position of the baht was placed above such national interests as economic development and stability of prices and incomes. The reason was partly to prevent foreign interference, partly the result of British advice, through British financial advisers. British policy sought order and stability in Thailand, and British traders a good market for exports. Seventy per cent of Thai imports (pre-war) came from Britain; Britain dominated banking and the production and sale of tin and teak. Thailand's liquid reserves, Ingram states, were tied up to meet the international obligations of foreign banks and bondholders. Irrigation projects were postponed and power neglected because of lack of funds.

war. Four big irrigation projects alone will add nearly a million tons of rice to Thailand's output.

Project	Date of Completion	Cost (million baht)	Irrigated Area (million rai)
Greater Chao Phya	1965	1,067	3·15
Yanhee	1964	730	—
Mae Klong	1968	900	2·3
Kampaengpet	1970	600	1·5

(From the Six Year Economic Plan (1961–67), cited by Bunchana Atthakor, Deputy Secretary-General, National Economic Development Board.)

The Chao Phya project is designed to allow double-cropping from Chainat to Ayuthaya, through an extensive canal system fed from the Chainat diversion dam. Of great importance is the Yanhee multi-purpose project, whose dam and reservoir will protect the Central Plain from floods and even out the water supply. It will also provide 560,000 kilowatts of badly needed electric power.

Highway construction and railway development also have immediate effects on production. Under the Six Year Plan a thousand kilometres of highways will be completed and another thousand kilometres of existing roads improved. The construction, maintenance and administration of roads amounts to over 40 per cent of total public investment, of which about half the cost has been paid in recent years by the Americans. The 1958 'Friendship Highway', opening up the North-East between Saraburi and Korat, is an outstanding example. In 1961 the 'East-West Highway', also built to American specifications, was opened to traffic between Pitsanulok and Lomsak. This road is intended, largely for strategic reasons, eventually to reach Nongkhai on the border of Laos. By 1962, the United States Operations Mission (USOM) will have rebuilt or replaced a thousand wooden bridges throughout the country.

Eleven years of American economic aid, starting in 1950, amount to 300 million dollars (American military aid is over 300 million). Over 2,400 Thai officials and professional workers have been trained abroad; fifty thousand teachers given further training in Thailand. More than fifty hospitals have been equipped; the death rate caused by malaria cut by 80 per cent. Four technical institutes have been set up to train over five thousand students.

Whereas Soviet aid to developing countries concentrates on 'spectacular' projects—a steel plant for India, an hotel for Burma, a hospital for Cambodia, nothing so far for Thailand—the United States spreads its aid widely on a whole series of basic improvements. This does not provide the immediate propaganda impact that the Russians achieve, but it has lasting value. Further, the Marxist insistence on industrialization, once so popular among the developing countries themselves, has lost ground before the basic demands of agriculture. Agriculture, on which the vast majority of the population depends, comes before steel mills—at least in South-East Asia—however attractive the latter may be in terms of national prestige.

The steady assistance sponsored by the Americans has its own productive reward, as illustrated by the following three examples. A farmer suffering from malaria can work only one or two hours in the morning and perhaps an hour in the late afternoon; free from it, he can work in the crop season all day. Improved varieties of rice can bring about a 15 per cent greater yield. Finally, tank irrigation in the North-East can help eradicate economic and, it is hoped, political discontent.

As for power, an American firm is constructing the great Yanhee hydro-electric and flood control project, which will vastly increase irrigation on the Central Plain and ultimately bring electric power to nearly half the provinces of Thailand. Present generating capacity is wholly insufficient. The total Thai consumption of electricity in 1956 was estimated at 18 to 20 kilowatt-hours a head, compared to 23 in India and 49 in Pakistan. Only half the capacity is produced publicly, the International Bank mission reports, the rest is generated privately by small and costly diesel units or by burning rice husks. Electric capacity at present is about 70,000 kilowatts in the provinces and 160,000 in Bangkok. Yanhee should provide a further 140,000 kilowatts by 1963, at a cost of 2,000 million baht—more than half covered by an International Bank Loan—and four times that amount of power twelve years later.

Education is of no less importance, both for its own sake, for the sake of responsible democracy, and for the sake of economic development.* Parallel to the Six Year Economic Plan for Thailand, the Minister of Education, Mom Luang Pin Malakun, has proposed a six year education programme. The emphasis is on primary and vocational education. Nine thousand teachers are to be trained every year, more than twice the present amount. More schools are to be built. In 1958, 415,000 children completed four years of primary education, but only 125,000 of them could go on to secondary schools. In that year, there were over four million pupils altogether, a ratio of one teacher to over thirty pupils and 150 pupils to a school.

	1950	*1958*
Schools	20,929	25,737
Teachers	84,735	121,132
Students	2,985,418	4,040,609
	(Bunchana Atthakor)	

Government expenditure on education is higher than in Burma, but far less than in Ceylon or the Philippines. It is the Japanese, with almost universal literacy, who have most clearly demonstrated the economic value of education.

Thai schools, unfortunately, show a high proportion of failures. Half of those in the first grade fail to complete their course, and so they repeat the entire course again. The obvious results, reports the International Bank mission, are laziness, overcrowding and a general slow-down of instruction. Since the end of the war, of every hundred who enter primary school, thirty-eight complete four years, eighteen (twenty-seven in 1961) enter secondary school, two finish the six-year course (while two enter vocational institutes), and only one goes to pre-university school. Over 70 per cent of teachers, since the end of the war, are untrained for their task; few of them have more than six-year secondary education, many only three years and some were only at primary school. The reasons for this poor quality are the low salaries offered, as well as the lack

* The economic significance of education was calculated thirty-five years ago by Strumilin, who showed that four years at a primary school increased a man's productive capacity by 44 per cent, a secondary education by 108 per cent and a university education by 300 per cent—Soviet delegate to UNESCO (*Guardian*, June 8, 1961).

of training colleges and instructors. These are the equivalents in sterling and dollars of figures cited by the mission:

Teacher (two years' college)	£90 a year	($270)
Graduate (College of Education)	£220 a year	($650)
Assistant lecturer (third grade)	£150–£240 a year	($450–700)
Lecturer (second grade)	£240–£460 a year	($700–1,350)
Professor (first grade)	£460–£730 a year	($1,350–2,150)

For the few with Western qualifications starting salaries are about double.

Such are civil service rates of pay—for teachers and professors in Thailand are all civil servants—and they are far below those paid in commerce and industry.

INDUSTRY

In private industry, the International Bank mission observed in 1958, the number of firms and establishments has doubled since 1950. Private construction has increased two or three times, the number of passenger and commercial vehicles four times. Whereas in 1950 there were only 1,750 plants regularly employing more than five workers each, and all were in Bangkok, ten years later there were 13,400 and nearly half were outside the capital. These are all light industries, as figures cited by the mission for 1957 indicate:

Industry	Establishments	Workers
Saw milling	1,736	130,154
Rice milling	4,921	58,459
Printing	484	17,288
Sugar milling	1,521	12,685
Weaving	409	12,470
Flour milling	1,336	11,982
Ceramics	90	11,694
Engine repair	528	7,219
Foundry and machine shops	810	6,931
Smithies	778	3,803
Ice factories	388	3,199
Soft drinks	143	1,946
Others	2,816	38,108

In fact, most of the rice and sugar mills employ seasonal labour—peasants who leave their fields once the crop is harvested; and saw millers include forest workers, charcoal burners and so on. Most of these establishments are owned by Chinese, though more and more of the unskilled labour, particularly up-country, is Thai.

Thailand lacks the basic fuel and metal resources for heavy industry: there are no coal deposits, a little oil (in the extreme North), some lignite, small deposits of iron ore. Manufacturing, mining and power altogether comprise only 15 per cent of the Gross National Product. Only 8 per cent of the economically active population, in 1960, were employed in industry (80 per cent in agriculture, forestry and fishing). But Government has ventured well beyond the field of irrigation and power. The manufacture of tobacco and playing cards are Government monopolies—and so, until recently, was whiskey distilling. The Government dominates production of timber (forest concessions have been nationalized), sugar, paper and gunny bags; and it has large interests in cement, glass, pharmaceuticals, batteries, tin, tanneries and textiles.

Government went into industry on the same tide of nationalist fervour shown by most Asian countries achieving independence after the end of the war. Results have not met expectations. 'The record of Government factories,' Ingram asserts, 'is not good. Perhaps corruption can be eliminated and efficient management achieved, but the experience to date is not encouraging. Investment expenditures have not been carefully supervised, schedules have not been met, production has been erratic, poor in quality, and far below capacity, losses have been common, and accounting has been inadequate.'

The International Bank report confirms the indictment—and adds to the schedule:

(a) Too often persons with political influence, but without specified knowledge, have initiated Government projects. There has been little control over expenditure.

(b) Fixed assets have been over-estimated. Supplies of suitable raw materials have not been assured, equipment is not always appropriate, managers are not always competent and marketing problems have been ignored.

(c) Assets and liabilities of the various ventures have been swollen by the practice of giving loans to, or borrowing from, other Government agencies—a 'pernicious system'.

(*d*) Managers and officials lack commercial experience; labour is idle, maintenance poor, operations inefficient.

(*e*) For political reasons a disproportionate number of workers have been taken on compared with private industry; this adds appreciably to high costs.

Government itself is not unaware of the problem—at least after the departure of Marshal Pibun. General Krit Punakan, then Minister of Industry, circulated to deputies (in July 1958) a list of 'Obstacles to Industrial Promotion'. These obstacles, which are worth giving in some detail, are:

(1) A benevolent nature which has made it unnecessary to work too hard for food and clothes, and hot weather which makes it difficult for enduring work.

(2) A sparse population, which results in lack of competition and lack of an adequate number of consumers to make establishment of certain industries worthwhile.

(3) A lack of technicians, which may be corrected by the Ministry of Education.

(4) Lack of the 'spirit of industrialism': industry needs the spirit of endurance to overcome obstacles, take risks of loss and wait for slow profits; without it, people take up the civil service and, where they have capital, lend money for interest and rent land and houses, in which the returns are quicker.

(5) Lack of proper long-term planning, a situation which the present (Thanom) Government is going to correct by drawing up economic projects.

(6) Inadequate budgetary allocation for the Ministry of Industry.

(7) Lack of public support for domestic manufacturers; 'faults have been found by people who fail to realize that industries in Thailand are like infants learning to walk and need assistance and encouragement'.

(8) Frequent changes of Government, resulting in lack of stable policy.

(9) 'Lack of understanding and co-operation between industrialists and Government offices, which results in unresolved arguments as to whether imports should be

prohibited to promote certain domestic industries or be allowed to continue to flow into the country, causing failure of the local factories.'

(10) Lack of adequate cheap power, which makes it necessary for industries to spend about 25 per cent of their capital to provide their own power. This will be corrected when the Yanhee Hydro-Electric project is completed.

(11) Obstacles concerned with foreign investment. . . . Thailand has the following disadvantages in this matter: (i) The population is too sparse to provide sufficient customers for certain industries. (ii) Loss of investment is feared, particularly if war breaks out. (iii) There is fear of uncertainty in Government policy. For example, the Ministry of Industry may have invited foreign investment in a certain industry requiring large capital. Protection should be given this industry, whose failure should not be brought about by the Government setting up a similar factory in competition. (This was a favourite practice of the former regime.)

All these obstacles—psychological and practical—exerted a baneful effect on Government business ventures during the Pibun regime. The biggest project—a group of new factories set up by the National Economic Development Corporation—was the worst failure. NEDC was set up with an authorized capital of fifty million baht (nearly £1 million or $2½ million), to finance the construction of, and to operate, two sugar refineries, a gunny bag factory (sacks for flour, rice, etc.), a paper mill and possibly a marble factory. At the end of 1957 (end of Pibun era) NEDC had a debt of over *six hundred* million baht: one sugar mill was making a small profit, the gunny plant was selling at heavy loss and the three other projects were unfinished.

The new Government discovered that only three million of the fifty million baht authorized capital had been paid up. Of the six hundred and fifty million baht in loans guaranteed by the Government, nineteen million had been lent to private concerns which had nothing to do with NEDC, a hundred and twenty-five million had been invested in the four factories and three and a half million used to build new offices (they already had a building). However, by May 1960, after a purge of high officials, work had started on the paper mill—debts had been reduced by nearly half to three hundred and sixty million—and it was expected to earn its way two years after completion (June 1961, later postponed to early 1962). One sugar mill had even lacked supply of raw materials, because it had been built in paddy country and the peasants resisted changing over to sugar cane; but it was now obtaining twice its previous income. Enough jute was also being produced to keep the gunny bag factory running. . . . This factory was the only one to make a profit in 1960: NEDC as a whole then reported a loss of thirteen million baht. By November 1961, both the North-East Jute Mills and the Chonburi Sugar Mill were making profits and NEDC had only 100 million baht of debts left unpaid. The Government stated that it was still willing to sell the various factories to private interests.

Among further discoveries made by the new regime was the misuse of funds by the Government Tobacco Monopoly. One million baht (from the workers' welfare fund) had been given for the personal use of Pibun; three million baht to the police for anti-Communist work; and twenty-two million lent various organizations without proper security. The Government Transport Company (it was learnt) had run up debts of forty-seven million baht and the National Audit Department found 'misconduct on the part of Company officials'. One of the first tasks of the new board of the Railways Organization (June 1959) was to deal with allegations of corruption and malpractices; the Minister of Communications had received twenty-five specific allegations by September. The Minister also had to investigate charges against the managing director of the Port of Thailand (Bangkok).

Merchants complained that if they did not pay 'tea money' they could not obtain official permits or facilities. As the newly appointed Finance Minister, Chote Gunakasem, added in February 1959, there was 'a lot of embezzlement' under the previous regime. Three months later he was himself arrested for allegedly receiving a commission (8 per cent) on a Government contract for printing bank notes.* Heavier penalties for crimes committed in an official or judicial capacity were

---

* The Criminal Court acquitted the defendant (December 28, 1961) because prosecution charges were 'not proven' and testimony was 'not sufficient' to find him guilty.

thereupon approved by the Constituent Assembly. Corruption cannot be eliminated from the scene, however, until the *phu yai* (big men) show a better example.

Thailand, fortunately, gets by on its agriculture. There are no serious problems of unemployment or lack of foreign exchange to create pressures for industrialization. But business initiative, states the International Bank mission, is not lacking. These are good opportunities in light engineering, textiles and assembly work. Chinese ownership is a complication, the report admits, but, assimilation provides the most hopeful solution. Above all, Government should disengage from its industrial ventures, develop basic facilities and encourage private, including foreign, investment.

The climate for investment in Thailand, concludes the survey carried out by George B. Beitzel and a number of leading American industrialists in November 1959, is 'fundamentally good'. But there needs to be an 'intensified effort to simplify Government procedures, to negotiate certain treaties affecting investment and to reduce Government participation in commercial enterprises'. The mission also recommended new investment legislation to set up a simple, legally constituted board of investment; better credit facilities to strengthen the position of the small Thai industrial entrepreneur; general improvement of management practices; and a blanket exemption from import duty for all productive machinery used in industrial enterprises, 'in order to provide a dramatic, universally available inducement which is entirely free of administrative discretion'.

The Beitzel survey urged that the Board of Investment draft an unequivocal policy statement for issuance by the Prime Minister emphasizing Government intention not to enter into enterprises of a commercial nature: 'An even greater demonstration of intent to remove uncertainties in this aspect of the investment climate would be systematic and vigorous action to dispose of as many existing Government-owned and operated enterprises as possible.'

In fact the Revolutionary Party had already pledged in December 1958 not to compete with private industry, nor to take over private enterprises. Machinery would be exempt from import duties; a two to five years 'tax holiday' would be allowed on sale of products; remittances abroad would be granted; and skilled workers and technicians would be permitted entry into Thailand irrespective of immigration quotas.

A Board of Investment under Tawee Bunyaket (formerly a supporter of Pridi, a Free Thai leader and once a Prime Minister for a few days) was set up in July 1959. But Tawee stated, in December 1960, that he was against extending to foreign investors all the privileges that the Malayan Government allowed. The Prime Minister, Marshal Sarit, was even more forthright. Thailand's neighbours were 'too lenient' with investors, he said. 'We don't want foreigners to become the masters of the business and industrial community here. We will stick to our policy of providing conditions under which a fair profit can be made on investment, but will remain the rulers of our own house.' This was in July 1960. A month before, he declared that would-be investors had only shown 'interest', not more. 'If the newspapers knew as much as I do,' he went on, 'they would be truly angry. Those who expressed interest in investment asked at first for protection. We have offered protection. They asked for a tax holiday. We have given them that. In the end they said that Communists are near Thailand and they want us to give the guarantee that Communism would not come to Thailand. Who can give such a guarantee? All we can say is that when Communism arises we shall suppress it. These people simply cause a headache.'

The Marshal had some reason for his exasperation. Apart from Communism, one big investment project had been cancelled, another had run into difficulties. Julio Munoz, Spanish promoter and head of an international finance group, had suggested planting a million *rai* of cotton in the North-East, then setting up a huge textile factory to make cloth. One and a half million people, said Sr Munoz, would be employed. But once the project was completed in twenty years (fifteen, said the Government), the Munoz Group said it would require complete control of all textile imports, for twenty-five years, except silks and woollens. (The Group would get a 2 per cent commission on imports, an income of about sixteen million baht a year.) The scheme sounded splendid, at first, until the implications of monopoly became clear. The deal was withdrawn.

The second problem was the Government request for an oil

refinery. The big oil companies all had refineries elsewhere and adequate means of transportation. But the Government, recalling wartime experience of being unable to import petrol, was insistent. Shell and Stanvac thereupon produced a joint proposal for a 35,000 barrels-a-day refinery in partnership with the Government, saving the latter 100 million baht a year in foreign exchange. The tiny Eastern Petroleum Company of Panama (backed by Standard Oil of Indiana) however won the contract in April 1959. The Company said it would construct a 28,000 barrels-a-day refinery, rent it from the Government for ten years and prohibit all other imports of petroleum. After lengthy negotiations with the Board of Investment, Standard Oil suddenly withdrew their offer in October 1960. Five months later, Shell announced that they would back the Thai Oil Refinery Company's offer to construct a 40,000-barrel refinery. Under new conditions imposed in July 1961, the offers both of Shell and of the Phillips Petroleum Company of New York were accepted, though the latter apparently withdrew. Signing the contract in September, Shell agreed to construct the refinery, at Siraja, within two years, at a cost of $30 million. After ten years of operation, handing over 25 per cent of profits—later extended to fifteen years—the refinery would be turned over to the Government.

A third big project, approved in May 1961, is for a 450 million baht textile plant employing ten thousand Thai workers, put forward by the Japanese Company Toyo Menka Kaisha. After ten years the plant would operate 100,000 spindles—in 1959 there were only 50,000 spindles and 20,000 weaving machines in the whole of Thailand—and would produce over 52 million pounds of yarn a year. Following protests by local weaving firms that the Japanese with their improved techniques would put them out of business, Toyo Menka agreed to reduce the numer of looms from 1,800 to only 400, similar to one of the larger Thai mills.

A better start was made with the Bangkok Jute Mill, scheduled to start production of fifteen million gunny bags a year within two years. Capitalized at forty million baht, the mill will employ 5,000 workers on three shifts. (Present production in Thailand is only nine million bags and twenty million more need to be imported every year from India or Pakistan.) Since

L

the Board of Investment began its operations in 1959, the Prime Minister stated in August 1961, 117 applications for investment with a total value of 1,800 million baht (£30 million or $90 million) have been approved. Of this total, about two-thirds comes from private foreign investors. Among them are pharmaceutical plants, German, US and Thai; an ironworks, Japanese-Thai; Bata shoes; Ever-Ready batteries; Nestlé tinned milk; Krupps blast furnace; American tyre factory; Thai nail and tinplate companies; and three car assembly plants for Fiats, English Fords and Japanese Nissan motors. The Thai Government in August 1961 accepted in principle a proposal by seven foreign firms, including Raymond International of America and two French companies, to build a free port and construct a canal through the Kra Isthmus—the narrowest part of the South Thailand peninsula. The Kra Canal Company, whose President is Pote Sarasin, state that exploration and survey will take two years and the actual construction work another seven. The proposal has long attracted the Thai Government, but it could not be realized before the war because of financial shortages and (British) political objections. The canal would cut shipping times—on present routes via Singapore—by three or four days.

The Government, for its part, proposes—in its Six Year Plan —to promote private investment in industries, particularly those which use locally available raw materials for a large part of their manufacture and those whose products are needed by domestic consumers in large quantities. Secondly, the Government will not establish any factory to compete with a private industry. Thirdly, it will promote geological research; fourthly, organize training of experts and technicians; and fifthly, promote home industries. Industrial income, which is increasing at the rate of 10 per cent a year, is to go up between 1961–63 by 12 per cent. Detailed percentage increases by 1963 will be:*

Cement	50	Paper	100	Tin ore	40
Textiles	100	Gunnies	50	Lignite	300
Sugar	8	Tobacco	50	Gypsum	300

* Actual production in 1960: cement about 900,000 tons; textiles 25·5 million lb.; sugar 110,000 tons; paper 2,500 tons; gunnies 5·8 million bags; tobacco 8,886 tons; tin 16,600 tons; lignite (1961) 114,000 tons. (Gypsum production, very small in 1957, increased fourfold by 1961.)

FINANCE

In the five years up to 1957, states the International Bank mission, total public expenditure increased by over 40 per cent (but more than 80 per cent of the country's total resources are still absorbed by the private sector). How is the Government to pay for the increased programme of highway development, irrigation and power projects, and more schools and teachers, envisaged under the Six Year Plan?

GROSS NATIONAL PRODUCT (1956)
(thousand million baht)

Agriculture, Forestry, Fishing	16·1
Wholesale and Retail Trade	8·0
Manufacture	5·3
Public Administration, Defence	2·4
Transport and Communications	2·3
Construction	1·4
Mining	0·7
Other Services	4·3
Expenditure (public sector)	
Consumption	4·4
Gross Fixed Investment	1·7
Expenditure (private sector)	
Consumption, including stock charges	29·4
Gross Fixed Investment	3·6
National Expenditure	39·1
plus Exports of Goods and Services	8·1
less Imports of Goods and Services	8·3
Gross National Product	38·9*

(From *A Public Development Program for Thailand*)

In the early years of the century, Ingram remarks, the largest single source of Government revenue was the profit from opium. With the profits also made from gambling, suppressed in 1905, they made up some 40 per cent of receipts. Import duties—kept at 3 per cent on all articles by treaty—

* GNP in 1961 increased to 50 thousand million baht, according to a statement by the Prime Minister in October 1961.

were less than 4 per cent of total revenue. Thailand made strenuous efforts to end foreign treaty concessions, including extra-territorial rights granted foreigners; by the end of the 'twenties import duties provided 13 per cent, and by 1950, 22 per cent of revenues. Income tax, introduced in 1941, was kept fairly low.

In 1957, nearly a fifth of total Government revenue came from the export tax on rice, about 6 per cent from taxes on rubber, tin and forestry exports. Income and business taxes provided 15 per cent of revenue, import duties about 24 per cent, and other indirect taxes 15 per cent. Total revenue was then 5,299 million baht (about £88 million, $260 million). In 1960 it was 6,540 million baht (£109 million, $325 million).

SIX-YEAR PLAN EXPENDITURES, 1961—66
(PERCENTAGES)

Economic Development	21
Education	17
Defence	17
Repayment of loans	15
Public health and welfare	11

(Total cost of the Plan—20,000 million baht.)

Substantial benefits are expected from the Plan and these gains will be reflected in increased revenue for the Government. At an average growth of 4 per cent a year, revenue is expected to increase from 7,100 million in 1961 to 9,500 million baht in 1966. Total expenditure, on the other hand, is to rise from 8,200 million in 1961 to 10,800 million in 1966. Internal loans are planned at over 1,000 million baht each year of the Plan, but the Government also counts on 4,000 million in foreign loans and 3,000 million in foreign aid, for the whole period, to help cover the deficit.

Besides the budget deficit, incurred because of development expenditure, Thailand for a number of years has experienced a deficit in the balance of payments. Thailand imports a great deal of capital equipment and consumer goods from Japan, America, Britain and Europe and her exports—almost entirely of raw materials, subject to fluctuations in world market prices —are insufficient to cover them. This trade gap has been met, in the past, by the use of American aid and by drawing on foreign exchange reserves: but the solution is more exports and better quality. This is now being achieved: in mid 1961, the trade gap was closed (temporarily) for the first time in seven years.

As is well known, the developing countries throughout the world tend to lose more from changes in the terms of trade than they can gain from foreign aid. As the *Bangkok Bank Monthly Review* (October 1961) puts it: 'The developed countries are at present helping us the wrong way. The volume of aid given to us is completely nullified whenever there is a minor fluctuation in the commodity prices. What we want is *trade and not aid* . . .' —in fact, action to ensure fair dealing, a market for products and relatively stable prices. Just as the weak are driven to the wall in a society where market forces operate unhindered, so the 'gap' between the poor and the prosperous countries of the world—between producers of raw materials and the industrialized countries dominating the world economy—this gap, so far from closing, gets wider every year.

MAIN IMPORTS 1960
(million baht)

Petroleum products	1,018
Iron and steel products	760
Cars, motor cycles	663
Cotton fabrics	637
Mining, construction, industrial machinery	554
Electric generators	501
Power generators	339
Milk products	359
Medical and pharmaceutical	320
Paper	264
Tyres and tubes	225
Others	3,833
Total imports	9,473
Total exports	8,629

(Bank of Thailand)

As for Thailand's budget deficit due to heavy development expenditure—expenditure rising from one-fifth to approaching one-third (28·7 per cent) of the total budget by the end of the

Plan—the International Bank indicates the 'urgent need' to increase the tax yield. The financial gap, according to its figures, was some 300 million baht in 1959 and would rise to about 900 million a year in the period 1961–63. (This 'gap' is to be covered, according to the Six Year Plan estimates, largely by internal loans on a much higher scale than those envisaged by the mission—four or five times more—which may be difficult to accomplish.) The present tax burden, the mission states, is only about 14 per cent of the Gross National Product. The proportion of direct taxation (about 7 per cent of revenue) is among the lowest in Asia. Tax evasion is commonplace. Family businesses, Ingram relates, have three sets of books to show: one for the tax collector, one for their own use, and the third, if the inspector is not satisfied, is the 'real account'. This recalls Pallegoix's story: 'Those who think of trading with Siam should bring three ships: one loaded with presents for the King and his ministers, another loaded with merchandise and the third loaded with patience.'

1962 BUDGET (ESTIMATE)

Income	million baht	percentage
Customs duty	2,948	32·2
Revenue tax	1,741	19·6
Rice export premium	730	8·2
Excise tax	590	6·6
State enterprises, agricultural products, industry, etc.	1,411	15·9
Loans	1,460	16·4
Total income	8,880	100

The mission admits the political difficulties involved in raising and enforcing additional taxation but makes these proposals:

(1) Revision of income tax scales and proper enforcement to double the tax yield in five years (350 million baht increase a year).

(2) Increased company taxes (50 million increase).

(3) Additional customs and excise dues, especially on petrol and luxury goods (200 million).

(4) Doubling the land tax rate—at present, in rural areas, about one baht a *rai*, a shilling or 15 cents an acre (50 million, for provincial revenues).

(5) Charges for the use of irrigation: 200 baht a *rai* for land which can be double cropped (50 million at first, about 150 million after 1963).

(6) Estate duty, or inheritance tax—at present non-existent— and heavier taxes on luxuries (50 million).

(7) Tax on property and other measures to give greater financial independence to municipalities (30 million, increasing to 120 million).

In Thailand there is no tax on owner-occupied houses or on real estate improvements (only on rented houses). But in most countries, the mission states, property taxes provide the major part of local revenues. At the moment, local development is 'grossly inadequate' in the supply of water, drainage, sewerage, transport, communications, power and housing. The efficiency of local administration needs greatly improving, but this is only possible, the mission says, if greater independence and responsibility are given to local authorities. However, past experience has not been encouraging. Local assemblymen, states W. D. Reeve in *Public Administration in Siam*, 'untrained in debate and inexperienced in public work of this nature, are often incompetent or worse. The electorate is apathetic; usually less than 5 per cent trouble to record their votes. . . .'

To what extent have the mission's proposals been adopted?

(1) Income taxes and sales taxes were raised in December 1959. Whereas previously incomes up to 100,000 baht (£1,650, nearly $5,000) were taxed at only 10 per cent, now the rate between 50,000 and 100,000 is 16 per cent, and between 10,000 and 50,000, 13 per cent. A Bureau for the Control of Taxation was set up in May 1960 to improve the work of tax collection. General Prapart, Minister of the Interior, at that time estimated that the Government should receive taxes from a quarter of the people, but he said only 14 or 15 per cent paid taxes.

(2) Company taxes, described as 'too low', were also revised in December 1959. Whereas 10 per cent was collected on net profits below 500,000 baht (£8,300, $25,000) now it is 15 per cent plus a straight tax of 1,000 baht for each

accounts period. Profits of over a million baht are taxed at 25 instead of 20 per cent. Trade taxes were also increased. Total direct taxation averaged 960 million baht a year in the three years up to 1958, but as much as 1,400 million baht a year in the following three years.

(3) A new specification of tariffs was adopted in March 1960, which would provide a further 60 million baht a year. (Total income from customs in 1960 came to about 2,300 million baht compared with an average of only 1,480 million a year from 1956–58). Fuel oil, but not kerosene— used by farmers—received more tax, but there has been no additional tax on luxury imports. From August 1961 all trade taxes were collected at the import and production end, on the advice of foreign tax experts who said that collection at source proved the only effective way of ensuring collection and preventing evasion. Four months later, the Minister of Finance pointed out that the Government was getting 'a most satisfactory increase in income'. He added that a thorough revision of the Revenue Code had been completed.

4) The nominal land tax remains unchanged. Rents for State lands, 'too unrealistically low' according to the Minister of Finance in April 1960, were to be raised. He said many of the lessees sub-let at the market rate and thus pocketed money which should have gone to the State. Income from public domains had almost doubled in the three years following the 1958 Revolution—amounting to 18 million baht in all—the Prime Minister reported in October 1961.

(5) The Irrigation Department announced in April 1962 that it would charge thirty baht per *rai* a year for supply of water, according to legislation being prepared.

(6) A Thai newspaper has raised the question of an inheritance tax, said to have existed before the war; but no official action has been taken.

(7) No property tax so far has been proposed; the munici-palities remain dependent on Government subsidies. At present, to put it frankly, they are part of the Government machine. The Lord Mayor of Bangkok, for example, is Director-General in the Ministry of the Interior.

The Prime Minister, in August 1960, ordered a halt to any

further increase in taxation for the next two years. The country, he said, was taxed to the fullest extent for the time being. Internal confidence in the financial situation could be proved, he pointed out in October 1961. Whereas in the three years before the Revolution the Bank of Thailand had to purchase nearly 400 million baht worth of Government bonds (out of 500 million) and the remainder was bought 'involuntarily' by the Government Savings Bank, State enterprises, the Red Cross, etc., in 1960 the Bank of Thailand had to take up only 16 million baht worth (out of 500 million) and in 1961 only three million—the rest being bought by commercial banks, insurance companies and the public.

All the same, the Minister of Finance urged people (in 1960) to save money, and not spend it, as is customary (and almost obligatory), on lavish weddings, parties and funerals. Some wedding gifts, he exclaimed, were so plentiful that lorries were needed to take them all away. Deposits in the Government Savings Bank (interest at 2½ per cent) had increased from 800 million to over 1,000 million baht in two years. But the Government bond issue for 500 million baht, repayable in fifteen years, received 8 per cent interest tax free. The Minister asked the Thai people to save, invest and work as hard as the Japanese did forty years ago to make their country one of the most advanced in the world.

Rates of interest, unfortunately, are low for savers; banks give 3 per cent, or 6 to 8 per cent at most. But they are high for commercial borrowers—as much as 2 per cent a month, or 24 per cent a year. Scarcity of capital is the reason as well as the lack of proper investment channels. There is no Stock Exchange in Thailand* and the people lack confidence in joint stock companies, states S. Y. Lee in the *Far Eastern Economic Review* of December 1, 1960 ('Currency, Banking and Foreign Exchange of Thailand'). These companies are not properly instituted: 'Business organizations among Chinese and Thai entrepreneurs remain on the family basis. Many joint stock companies exist in name only.' Lee goes on:

'People who have money may purchase gold to hoard, speculate in land and houses, which if not effectively used can be regarded as inactive investment, or deposit money in

* A stock exchange, on a limited basis, was started in June 1962.

banks. . . . Worst of all, some very rich people resort to capital flight by remitting money abroad to Switzerland, the United States and Hong Kong. As business savings such as reserves and undivided dividends, and Government savings from budgetary operations, are insignificant, the supply of savings funds comes mainly from private individuals.'

Thai national income is low, Lee adds, and the propensity to save of people with a taste for luxury imports is also low. The amount is far from enough to finance investment.

Yet if savings are still low, and if taxation cannot easily be raised (for political reasons), at least the present Government has greater control over economic development and financial management. 'It was not until the Revolutionary Government that orderly and planned economic development was worked out,' declared the Minister of Finance, Sunthorn Hongladarom, to the deputy editor of the *Far Eastern Economic Review* (July 21, 1960). Capital projects of the eighty or more 'independent Government agencies', which formerly received and spent large sums unrecorded in the budget, are now subject to the survey and approval of the National Council for Economic Development. Some of these agencies—among them are the Tobacco Monopoly, State Railways, Port Authority, Express Transport Organization, Fuel Oil Organization and State Savings Bank—send in part of their income as revenue to the State. In general, the Minister added, they have become more 'co-operative'.

Budget procedure, once 'grossly inadequate', has markedly improved. A Budget Bureau, working directly under the Prime Minister, was formed in 1959 to collect budget estimates from various departments and to recommend allocations of funds. The Bureau is responsible for drafting the budget and presenting it to the Cabinet for approval. A National Council for Economic Development (also proposed by the International Bank) was appointed in July 1959, with the Prime Minister in the Chair, Generals Thanom and Prapart with Prince Wan as Vice-Chairman and a nine-member Executive Board.* The

* Members are Pote Sarasin, Secretary-General of SEATO, former Prime Minister; Tawee Bunyaket, Chairman of the Board of Investment; Mom Luang Dej Sanitwong, Chairman of the Economic Advisory Board of the Revolutionary Party; Air Marshal Phra Vejjayant Rangsit, Chairman of the Thai Technical and Economic Committee (co-operating with US aid officials); Puey Eungpakorn, Governor of the Bank of Thailand, former Director of the Budget Bureau; Lt

Council, with forty-five members, was granted wider functions in June 1960. It now considers the plans and projects of ministries, departments and Government enterprises and co-ordinates them for long-term development, according to available resources and priorities. After consulting officials, it recommends various allocations for ministries and departments. It surveys and checks the actual expenses compared with budget allotments. It surveys and reports on the results of the economic development projects of the various ministries and recommends that they be expedited, revised and suspended or cancelled as it thinks fit.

Administration at the highest level is thus ensured. But there is a great shortage of trained men, states the International Bank report, to carry out decisions. Although Government financed the education abroad of some two thousand Thais in 1957 (and three to four thousand more were trained under American, United Nations and Colombo Plan technical assistance programmes), too much stress was set on academic degrees, without regard for the quality of the university or institution, or for the practical experience and skill of the trainee. It is a great disservice, the mission points out, to lower standards of education for foreign students (as has happened in some American universities). Their countries desperately need high quality. 'It would be better both for Thailand, and for the individual student, for him to fail an examination than fail later on the job.'

Nor are trained men well used when they return. Job descriptions are virtually non-existent. 'A large proportion of Thais trained abroad end up in positions for which they are either under-qualified, over-qualified, or entirely unsuited.' It is common form to meet well-trained and enthusiastic young men, anxious to put into practice what they have learned abroad, yet unable to make any impression on their seniors; by the time they have reached a position of authority, it is too late. The results of appointing inexperienced managers to run Government enterprises, the mission points out, is 'almost

General Chitti Navisathien, former Deputy Economic Minister; Rear Admiral Chalee Sinthusophon, Under-Secretary for Industry; Leng Srisomwong, former Governor of the Bank of Thailand; and Chalong Peungtrakul, Secretary-General of the Council.

uniformly bad'. The habit of passing all questions upwards for a decision causes long delays and an inordinate volume of work to be handed on to the Cabinet, much of which could be settled by heads of departments. Finally, low pay. Low pay and poor promotion greatly contribute to low morale, slackness and inefficiency in the civil service. The level of pay is only one-half or one-third that of comparable occupations in private industry. A cost of living adjustment was made in 1952, but it was soon overtaken by inflation. This is the most serious and pressing problem. Firstly, the number of people employed should be reduced (if only by not replacing those who retire).* Secondly, pay and prospects should be improved. Then, thirdly, strong action should be taken against inefficiency and abuse. Good pay and suppression of corruption vastly improved the work of the British East India Company. There is no reason why they should not do the same in Thailand.

---

* Sixty per cent of the budget goes to pay the salaries of Government officials. The Minister of Finance announced in December 1961 that he would put a 'moratorium' on taking in new officials, except for teachers in Government schools and doctors in Government hospitals. Official salaries are still 'relatively low', Marshal Sarit admitted in February 1962. 'Low salaries are a cause of corruption', but though he would like to raise them, 'where is the money to come from?'

CONCLUSION

Thailand has no grandiose landscapes and not much picturesque scenery; it is a land, not of nobility and awe, but of unusual charm: winding canals flanked by trees, overhanging bamboos and huts on piles; children splashing, women bathing; floating stores, coffee boats, rice-laden vessels and lines of barges under tow; the brilliant green fields of rice newly planted, flame trees flowering in the hot season, the yellows and browns of dried bamboos; children riding the broad backs of buffaloes, rows of peasants harvesting the grain; the great wall of the Grand Palace, the classic perfection of the Marble Temple, golden Doi Suthep near Chiangmai; the breeze of evenings, the clear stars, comforting warmth; the temple fairs, the bright lights and music of Chinese streets, business in Yawarad day and night.

Life is near to nature. Houses are barely furnished, but airy, though windows in town are often screened against mosquitoes and shuttered against thieves. Outside, grass, creepers, bamboos, banana plants, palms and trees grow profusely. 'What a contrast,' writes Henri Mouhot, the French naturalist and explorer, 'between this nature and that of Europe! Compared to this flaming globe, this sparkling sky, how pale is our sun, how cold and sombre our skies! How fine it is, in the morning, to rise before the glowing sun! And still finer in the evening, to listen to a thousand sounds, metallic and strident cries, arising from all points of the earth. . . .'

So it was a hundred years ago, when Mouhot travelled on foot, by boat and on elephant back through Siam; so it is today. But the sounds of frogs and insects now mingle with radio music in the shops, popular songs relayed along Bangkok's main avenue, transistors among the market stalls and vans loudly advertising films. The *douceur* of evening is sweetened still more by the communal TV set, the coloured fountains and the neon lights.

Bangkok youth today views American movies in air-conditioned cinemas, reads lurid magazines, drinks soft drinks, wears hawaii shirts and says the inevitable 'O.K.' Middle-class houses have refrigerators, offices (more and more) air-conditioning. Modern men and women play golf or tennis, swim in the sea, water-ski on the river. Commercials fill the air, Thai music is transformed into lilting 'pops', rock 'n' roll rivals the *ramwong*. Thai classical dancers, in their gold crowns and gorgeous brocade, pose for photographers or perform at night clubs. (The Fine Arts Theatre, with its genuine displays, was burnt down one night in November 1960, but shows go on at the 'Culture Hall'.) Even the boxers, traditionally Thai (feet, knees, arms and elbows), are announced as 'willowy poisonous tornado, terrific rooted deed and dynamic'.

But do not regret the rapid pace of change, which has brought bicycles and buses to villagers, radio and electricity to isolated places, and health and the amenities of life to so many.* Despite Western contagion (often the worst of influences) a truly-rooted culture will survive—or be born again.

*   *   *

Like traditional culture, religion (or rather the practice of religion) has become attenuated, especially in towns. Few now regularly attend temple services, except the old and ailing. But tolerance, peacefulness, the aversion from violence, argument or taking life—these remain, though how much they are due to religion, to an 'attractive and undemanding environment' (noted by the International Bank) or to racial characteristics, who can say? There are discrepancies indeed: Thais are thin-skinned, dislike criticism and in a fit of passion can strike down a wife or friend, such as in the following incident.

---

* Not everyone would agree with this. 'When they passed one of these Laotian villages that had always enchanted him,' writes Norman Lewis in *A Single Pilgrim*, 'he thought of the cinema it would soon have, and then later, as progress took root, the saloon with the pin-tables and the juke-box, then the motor roads coming— the discovery perhaps of mineral resources, the factory poisoning the river, the forests pulped to feed the voracious ignorance of mass-education. . . .' Pristine innocence corrupted by Western materialism: there is some truth in that, but it is also something of a myth. Tourists in the same way prefer picturesque squalor—in markets or villages—to order and cleanliness, which they are used to in their own countries. But what of the inhabitants themselves? It is they, after all, who want pin-tables and cinemas, or there would be no point in installing them. You cannot isolate people from such things, or preserve them in the past. What would be Indian civilization, which we so much admire, without the rude invasions of the Aryans, or the Turks or the Moguls? Or Japanese culture without the massive influence of China? Thailand herself is the product of both these forces and she is changing still.

Nai Pao returned to his house in Onuch Lane, Phra Khanong, yesterday afternoon, found his brother-in-law, Nai Chamras, drunk, scolded him and, when Nai Chamras shouted back at him, ordered him out of the house. Nai Chamras seized a knife, stabbed Nai Pao many times, and then walked out of the house.

This is 'face'. Only violence can undo the overwhelming sense of shame—of ridicule or humiliation—which is loss of face. Junior officers and men have been known to kill their superiors on receiving a reprimand. Junior wives have shot their husbands; jealousy too springs from loss of face. A Minister of Agriculture was killed not long ago and the Prime Minister had to appeal to junior wives, in the national interest, not to shoot Government servants. Fear of losing face—which is not unknown in the West—inhibits, or at least obscures, initiative. Intermediaries are widely used to avoid either giving or taking offence: thus the principal is absolved from any formal responsibility.

Feelings still have direct expression and are not repressed, as in the West; the result is more bloodshed, less neuroses. Shame, rather than sin, matters in the East. A cheerful, friendly, casual nature takes little account of remorse or guilt. The Buddhist believes that bad deeds must work themselves out, that good deeds will be rewarded. Couples who commit suicide for love are sure they will be happy, together, in their future life. Indeed, funerals in Thailand are not sad or gloomy. This is due partly to belief in reincarnation and a sense of destiny (*karma*); partly to the cremation ceremony itself, which may take place weeks for ordinary people, months for the aristocracy, or years, in the case of royalty, after death; and partly to natural high spirits.

Thais have their worries, indeed, but essentially they are practical and down-to-earth. They have little aptitude for theory, no great intellectual curiosity—one disadvantage of life in Thailand. Outside the popular or classical theatre there are no plays and few concerts or good films. Radio is commercial, reading marginal (books or newspapers) and there is TV. Conversation is agreeable, but not critical. There is a pervading, luxuriant, passivity.

Perhaps this explains the passion for gambling—an interlude

of genuine excitement. More probably, as in the West, it is the lure of immense and unworked-for gain. There are other recreations, notably drink and women (*Mekhong* advertises a beautiful girl bending over a glass of their whiskey), which are well provided; but the greatest are rest and relaxation.

Leisure springs from the soil. For Thailand's rice economy is based on a few months' hard work—planting, weeding, harvesting and threshing—and the rest of the year is largely free. There are few needs in a warm, gentle climate; there is enough to eat and to spare. In such an environment there is little demand for 'enterprise'—or indeed for Communism—which in any case is provided by foreigners or overseas Chinese. Thais themselves prefer work on the land or in Government offices. They share the traditional Asian contempt for merchants. (In feudal society, priest, warrior and farmer ranked before the artisan, and the merchant came last of all.) Thus inertia tends to spread, as well as nepotism and corruption (both enemies of enterprise), to the administration as well.

Hence the strictures—'tenacious' adherence to traditional practices, 'grossly inadequate' budgeting—of the International Bank mission. These criticisms, set beside the recognition of considerable progress and great potentialities, are not academic; they are intended to force awareness of the fact of change and of the pressures from without. Thailand is less and less a subsistence country unaffected by the world. Competition for markets, a growing population, international uncertainties, all compel a new and modern outlook. And the impact of these on Government, which is clearly in evidence, has its effect on society as well.

Within this century the Thai ruling class has already widened, from the king and immediate royal family to high ranking officers and officials. But it still goes no further—actual power has been displaced rather than diffused—than the aristocracy, the wealthy and the influential. Public opinion, as distinct from nationalism, is almost non-existent. For the middle class is weak, divided as it is between the lower ranks of the Army, administration and professions, who are Thais, and the lesser businessmen, who are almost entirely Chinese. At the base stands an undemanding peasantry, isolated in its forty thousand villages, and a small and disorganized proletariat, again chiefly Chinese.

Coups d'état are the expression of the instability of personal rule, as of rule by narrowly-based cliques. In this way, change is brought about, not by the desire of the people's representatives, or through constitutional procedures, or for any good reason, but at the will of the few and by force. Authority is not diffused throughout the community. There is no real civilian control, for power must be exercised directly, in defence of the country it is true, but also, and patently, in self-defence.

Now the changing economic situation cannot fail to have its effect on the vagaries of politics. Economic progress creates a stronger middle class simply by producing large numbers of trained personnel (managers, technicians, skilled workers). The influence they are able to bear clearly expands in proportion as development itself assumes growing national significance.

It is pleasant to surmise that the new 'climate' of improvement sponsored by Marshal Sarit (himself a beneficiary of the *coup* system) will have the effect of transforming personal rule and the politics of *coups* into a more broadly-based and perhaps even parliamentary regime. But it will take time to develop the necessary code of behaviour. Until the administration is better paid, the public better informed, and both more responsive, self-government will remain an empty shell.

Certainly the existence of an authoritarian and (in part) corrupt regime* is dissatisfying—sometimes deeply so—to many in the educated middle classes. But this type of government is immaterial to the mass of the people so long as (*a*) it removes grievances and (*b*) leaves people alone. Trouble comes when discontent is suppressed (instead of its causes being examined and remedied) which may still be the case in the North-East; and when, often for the sake of 'tidiness'—as with the recent banning of hawkers from many streets and lanes, the warnings against 'loafing' in coffee-shops, etc.—people start to

* An observer complains of 'rampant' corruption—notably in high military circles—police extortion and frequent 'shady' provincial governors: 'big business in the nastiest sense battens upon the body politic, so that often a stroke of national policy is dependent upon the interests of a particular big-wig.' James Morris, 'Snags in Siamese Paradise', in the *Manchester Guardian Weekly*, February 1 and 8, 1962.

M

get 'pushed around'. It is then that the need for democracy, which allows grievances to be properly aired and popular viewpoints felt, becomes most obvious.

* * *

Thailand is no less mature than her neighbours. Burma, Malaya, Cambodia and the Philippines have all held relatively free and fair elections. Indeed it was the military regime in Burma that provided for its own parliamentary successor. Opposition parties are represented in all these assemblies, except in Cambodia where they failed to win a single seat. Yet there is a difference, and it is an important one. Thailand alone in South-East Asia was never subject to colonial rule.

This cuts both ways. In Thailand there is no feeling of inferiority, no constraint over 'colonialism' or 'imperialism', but a delightful sense of ease and fellowship. But since there was no colonialism, no national movement in the towns and villages could grow and struggle to oppose it. The ordinary man in the street—still less the peasant farmer—took no part in the *coup* which ended absolute monarchy; it was merely a change, and rather a disturbing change, of leadership at the top. There was no progress from nationalism to national participation, and hence no real democracy. Ironically, Thailand did improvise her own 'colonial' system—a half-nominated, half-elected legislature—but failed to develop from there.

Democracy in Asia faces four problems: the disinterest of the peasantry; the power of the military; the existence of corruption; and the danger of subversion. The ignorance and apathy of the great majority of the people are fatal to the democratic process, for they feel no need to defend it when it is threatened. Only if the politics of the city becomes the policy of irrigation, road building, agricultural research, marketing and credit facilities will democracy be worth defending.

Traditionally the Army has taken over where democracy has failed. But it is the hardest thing to stand aside and let it try again. Ideally the Army should permit the free play of forces— political, press, labour—to develop within society: the Army should only hold the ring. But this is an important function, to preserve the basic rules. No one can begrudge the Army stepping in, as it had to in Burma and Pakistan, when the State virtually broke down.

Why did the system break down? In the case of Burma it was the threat of subversion: a minority Government, dependent on pro-Communist support, was struggling against open Communist and other rebellions.* In the case of Pakistan, it was economic and political inefficiency, corruption and decay: freedom without social responsibility had turned sour. Paradoxically, leadership (like that of Nehru, Prince Sihanouk, even U Nu) is needed to inspire trust in democracy, while the leader is kept within constitutional bounds by the pressure of popular forces he has himself aroused. Factionalism, self-seeking, is the curse of Asian democracy; but a dynamic, personal relationship between leader and led can keep the system going until a tradition of democratic choice has formed.

A dilemma faces all Asian countries: the open society is good in theory, but is it possible? Where can one draw the line between criticism and subversion? Can any Thai Government, for example, allow freedom of speech and press, and free labour and student unions, if one section bitterly attacks the US commitment and the SEATO alliance? It is an answer to point out, however, that the attractions of a free society do outweigh the appeals of Communism. Communism for those who lead it is an ideal, and it should be countered—before traditions lose their strength—by a better ideal.

*   *   *

Is this the alternative? Who can say how the internal and external pressures on a country will turn out? In the short term, in Thailand, if the Prime Minister goes (through ill-health), the more forceful of his Army deputies, General Prapart—a nationalist, with a well-developed instinct for commerce—may be expected to take command. It is too early to speak of a return to real civilian rule—though men of ability and integrity are not lacking. However the Army is not a monolith. The younger officers, particularly those trained abroad, may press

* Ne Win's second *coup*, in March 1962, was to prevent the country breaking up, as he believed, into separate regions, owing to the uncontrolled activities of Shan and other chieftains and the general weakness of U Nu's administration.

for more liberalism, or socialism—at least state socialism. In the long term, the international balance of power is the decisive factor. If or when China regains her ascendancy, and America loses it, South-East Asia will enter—as Prince Sihanouk has predicted—the Chinese orbit. The length of time this takes— and the disposition of the countries concerned—may make all the difference between a tyrannical or a benevolent authority. One can only hope for the best.

IMPORTANT DATES

6th Century B.C.	Life of the Buddha
7th Century A.D.	Mon Kingdom, Dvaravati (central Thailand)
	Thai Kingdom, Nanchao, Yunnan (S.W. China)
11–12th Centuries	Thai tribes migrate south; zenith of Khmer Empire (Cambodia, Thailand)
1113–50	Suryavarman II, founder of Angkor Wat
1253	Kublai Khan conquers Nanchao
1283–1317	Rama Kamheng, King of Sukhotai, originates Thai alphabet, sends mission to Emperor of China

AYUTHAYA

1350	Founding of Ayuthaya
1448–88	King Trailok, administrative and legal reforms
1518	Portuguese mission to Ayuthaya
1569	Burmese capture Ayuthaya
1590–1605	King Naresuen kills Burmese Crown Prince, suzerain over Cambodia
1605–10	King Ekatosarot: Japanese mercenaries (Yamada, captain of the King's Bodyguard); Netherland's factory
1612	East India Company factories
1657–88	King Narai, poet, patron of letters
1685	Mission of Louis XIV (Chevalier de Chaumont)
1688	Phaulkon executed, death of King Narai, French expelled
1767	Burmese destroy Ayuthaya: General Taksin repels Burmese; King (at Thonburi)
1778	Capture of Vientiane, Emerald Buddha taken at Siam
1782	General Chakri proclaimed King (Bangkok); Taksin executed

BANGKOK

1785–87	Nguyen Anh (later Emperor Gialong of Vietnam) in Bangkok

1788	Buddhist Council revises canon
1805–08	Revision of Law Code
1824–26	First Anglo-Burmese War (ends Burmese threat to Siam
1827	Lao Prince revolts; Thais occupy Vientiane
1835	First printing press set up by American missionaries
1837	Reformed Buddhist sect founded by Prince Mongkut
1839–42	British defeat China in Opium War (deep effect on Siam)
1851	Accession of King Mongkut
1855	Bowring Treaty of Friendship and Commerce (British trade, extra-territorial concessions): 'a total revolution in all the financial machinery of the Government', Sir J. Bowring
1856–68	Treaties with France, USA, Denmark, Portugal, Netherlands, Prussia, Belgium, Italy, etc.
1862	Charoen Krung (New Road) built
1868	Accession of King Chulalongkorn
1871	First royal visit abroad (Singapore and Java) in nearly 300 years
1874–1905	Abolition of slavery
1880's	End of traditional junk trade with China; European steamers predominant
1892–99	Rolyn Jacquemins (former Minister of Interior, Belgium) General Adviser to the King
1893	French gunboats blockade Bangkok; Luang Prabang ceded to France
1894–97	Criminal and Civil Courts established
1896	Bangkok-Ayuthaya railway (1900 to Korat, 1921 to Chiangmai, 1922 link with Malaya)
1901	First Thai budget
1903	Van der Heide's twelve-year irrigation plan shelved
1907	Angkor Wat, four provinces ceded to France
1908	Land Act: right to as much as each can use (eight to twenty acres): Founding of Chinese Chamber of Commerce
1909	Four Malay sultanates renounced
1910	King Vajiravud, Failure of Chinese general strike
1917	War against Germany. Chulalongkorn University founded
1921	Compulsory education decreed
1925	King Prajadiphok
1932	Promoters' *Coup:* End of Absolute Monarchy

MODERN ERA

1933	Phya Bahon Prime Minister. Col Pibun crushes royalist revolt
1935	Prajadiphok abdicates
1938	Pibun Prime Minister
1939	Restrictions on Chinese
1941	Alliance with Japan, seizure of parts of Burma, Laos and Cambodia
1942-43	Construction of 'death railway' to Burma
1944	Pridi in power. Return of seized territories (1944-46)
1946	Death of King Ananda
1947	November: Army *coup* restores Pibun. Pridi flees.
1949	February: abortive plot by Pridi. Chinese immigration quota reduced to 200 a year .
1950	US military and economic aid agreement
1951	June: Navy revolt; three days fighting. November: 'Insiders' *Coup*'; Phao Dep. Minister of Interior, Sarit Dep. Minister of Defence
1952-54	Communist plots, arrests, especially of Chinese
1955	April-June: Pibun's world tour: 'democracy'. SEATO Headquarters established. Imports from China allowed
1957	February: controlled elections. September 16: Pibun and Phao ousted. December: Pote Sarasin caretaker Government. December 15: elections. General Thanom Prime Minister
1958	March: Twenty-six by-elections (Democrats win fourteen). July: US 'Friendship Highway', Saraburi to Korat, opened. October 20: Sarit's Revolution; martial law, Constitution abolished, parliament dissolved, Communists arrested. November: dispute with Cambodia
1959	January: Ban on trade with China. February: Constituent Assembly; Sarit Prime Minister. April: Board of Investment. July: ban on opium smoking. National Economic Development Corporation
1960	June: Royal visit to America and Europe (return January 1961)
1961	March: US 'East-West Highway'. May-July and December: North-East conspirators arrested. October: Six Year Economic Plan starts. November: second dispute with Cambodia

1962   Five Year Development Plan for the North-East.
         March 6: US–Thai joint statement. May: US troops
         land in Thailand

BOOKS ON THAILAND

BLOFELD, JOHN. *People of the Sun: Encounters in Siam*, Hutchinson, 1960
BUSCH, NOEL. *Thailand: an Introduction to Modern Siam*, D. Van Nostrand Co Inc, 1959
CHAUMONT DE. *Relation de l'Ambassade de Mr le Chevalier de Chaumont à la Cour du Roy de Siam*, Paris, 1686
CHULA-CHAKRABONGSE. *Lords of Life*, Alvin Redman, 1960
COAST, JOHN. *Some Aspects of Siamese Politics*, mimeo., Institute of Pacific Relations, 1953
CROSBY, JOSIAH. *Siam: the Crossroads*, Hollis and Carter, 1945
DE YOUNG, JOHN. *Village Life in Modern Thailand*, University of California Press, 1955
GRAHAM, W. A. *Siam*, de la More Press, 1924
HRAF (Editor Wendell Blanchard). *Thailand: Its People, its Society, its Culture*, Human Relations Area Files, New Haven, 1957
IBRD. *A Public Development Program for Thailand*, International Bank for Reconstruction and Development, John Hopkins University Press, 1959
INGRAM, JAMES C. *Economic Change in Thailand since 1850*, Stanford University Press, 1955
LANDON, K. P. *Siam in Transition*, University of Chicago Press, 1939
MACDONALD, ALEXANDER. *Bangkok Editor*, Macmillan, 1949
MOUHOT, HENRI. *Voyages dans les Royaumes de Siam, de Cambodge, de Laos*, Paris, 1868
PALLEGOIX, MGR. *Description du Royaume Thai, ou Siam*, Paris, 1854
REEVE, W. D. *Public Administration in Siam*, Royal Institute of International Affairs, 1951
SKINNER, WILLIAM G. *Chinese Society in Thailand: an analytical history*, Cornell University Press, 1957
WOOD, W. A. R. *History of Siam*, Bangkok, 1926

NEWSPAPERS (English language)

BANGKOK POST. Editor: Harry Frederick
BANGKOK WORLD. Editor: Darrell Berrigan
SIAM RATH WEEKLY. Editor: Kukrit Pramoj

BOOKS ON SOUTH-EAST ASIA

BRIMMEL, J. H. *Communism in South-East Asia: a political anaylsis*, Oxford University Press, 1959
HALL, D. G. E. *A History of South-Eas Asia*, Macmillan, 1955

LE MAY, REGINALD. *Cultural History of South-East Asia: the heritage of India*, Allen & Unwin, 1954

PURCELL, V. W. V. S. *The Chinese in South-East Asia*, Oxford University Press, 1951

TRAGER, F. N. (ed.). *Marxism and South-East Asia*, Rand Corporation, 1957 (Stanford University Press, 1959)

BUDDHISM

HUMPHREYS, CHRISTMAS. *Buddhism*, Penguin Books, 1951

PERCHERON, MAURICE. *Buddha and Buddhism*, Longmans, 1957

THOMAS, E. J. *The Road to Nirvana*, John Murray, 1950

OTHERS

COEDES, GEORGES. *Pour Mieux Comprendre Angkor*, Adrien Maisonneuve, Paris, 1947

LATOURETTE, K. S. *The Chinese: their history and culture*, Macmillan, 1956

INDEX

GEORGE ALLEN & UNWIN LTD

London: 40 Museum Street, WC1

Auckland: 24 Wyndham Street
Bombay: 15 Graham Road, Ballard Estate, Bombay 1
Bridgetown: P.O. Box 222
Buenos Aires: Escritorio 454-459, Florida 165
Calcutta: 17 Chittaranjan Avenue, Calcutta 13
Cape Town: 68 Shortmarket Street
Hong Kong: 44 Mody Road, Kowloon
Ibadan: P.O. Box 62
Karachi: Karachi Chambers, McLeod Road
Lahore: Nawa-I-Waqt Building, 4 Queens Road
Madras: Mohan Mansions, 38c Mount Road, Madras 6
Mexico: Villalongin 32-10, Piso, Mexico 5, D.F.
Nairobi: P.O. Box 4536
New Delhi: 13-14 Asaf Ali Road, New Delhi 1
Ontario: 81 Curlew Drive, Don Mills
Phillippines: 7 Waling-Waling Street, Roxas District, Quezon City
Sao Paulo: Caixa Postal 8675
Singapore: 36c Prinsep Street, Singapore 7
Sydney, N.S.W.: Bradbury House, 55 York Street
Tokyo: 10 Kanda-Ogawamachi, 3-Chome, Chiyoda-Ku

AFRO-ASIAN STATES AND THEIR PROBLEMS

K. M. PANIKKAR

Between 1945 and 1957 many states in Asia and Africa achieved independence. India, Pakistan, Burma, Indonesia, Ceylon, Vietnam, Cambodia and Laos emerged from their colonial position and became sovereign states. In the Middle East there were similar developments with Syria and the Lebanon, while the Sudan became independent and the French withdrew from Tunisia and Morocco. Lastly in 1957 Ghana achieved Dominion status.

The problems faced by these countries are in many ways similar. They have had in every case to build up a political organization, to provide the administrative services necessary for a modern government and their economy has had to be reorganized.

In this book which is based upon a series of lectures delivered at the Institut d'Etude de Development Economique et Social in Paris Mr Panikkar examines the many problems involved and indicates ways to their solution.

Crown 8vo. 12s 6d net

EAST ASIA: THE GREAT TRADITION

E. O. REISCHAUER and J. K. FAIRBANK

A broad and interpretive account, this book is divided according to the main geographical-cultural areas. More than half deals with the development of China and its contacts with the nomadic peoples to the north. A small section tells the story of Korea, constituting what is actually the first account of Korean history in any Western language that goes beyond the bare bones of chronological, political history. The rest of the book deals with Japan.

The strong points of the book are: 1. the overall picture it gives of institutional and cultural growth; 2. the balance and integration between economic, political, intellectual and cultural factors (rarely attained in other books on Chinese history); 3. the fruitful comparisons and relationships it draws between historical developments in the major East Asian countries and also between them and the rest of the world; and 4. a number of new concepts and interpretations which give new meaning to many aspects of East Asian history.

What is extremely important is that the authors have approached their study of East Asia as the people of this area see themselves—'in historical perspective . . . the first requisite for understanding', thus providing a clear outline of the achievements of these peoples during their long period of semi-isolation from the rest of the world and a key to that awareness of the traditional culture which is 'essential to any comprehension of what is happening in East Asia today'.

Small Royal 8vo. Illustrated. 63s net

THE ASIAN CENTURY

PROFESSOR JAN ROMEIN

Translated from the German by R. T. CLARK

The last hundred years have seen the transformation of Asia. In the north Russia has absorbed the old Moslem states and has civilized Siberia; in the south-east and south-west former 'colonial' territories—the Middle East under Turkey, India and Ceylon under Britain, Indo-China under France, and Indonesia under the Dutch—are now free and independent. China is now Communist; old countries like Persia and Siam have entered the mainstream of international life; Turkey is a secular republic; Japan's bid for empire has failed; and Britain has abandoned Egypt to an ambitious dictator.

Asia has also suffered a social and industrial revolution which is still in progress. This development has been followed with passionate interest by a Dutch historian, Professor Romein, who knows south-east Asia at first hand. His book is mainly concerned with this area, but he includes also Turkey, China and Japan. He sees the revolution under a variety of aspects, initially as a struggle against 'colonialism' and a reaction against the West, seen as much in imitation as in resistance to its domination. Each country's answer to the problems confronting it is carefully analysed, whether arising from the desire for independence or from the onset of the great technological changes of our times whereby nations moved from a peasant to an industrial economy, changes which coincided in time with the revelation of Western weakness in two World Wars.

Professor Romein sees the Asian century as over in the sense that Asia is now free of foreign domination, a victory which has created more problems for the new states than it has solved. Asia is still 'on the march' to a future which it is difficult to foresee. If Professor Romein is frankly 'anti-colonial', he is equally frank about those who in Asia led the fight against it and have now the full responsibility for what he sees as a race against time. No one who is aware of the importance of Asia in the contemporary world can neglect his account of an astounding transformation accomplished in relatively so short a time. In it not only can the past be studied but the possible endings to a time of troubles which is by no means over. On what ending is made, the future of the world largely depends.

Demy 8vo. 50s net

JOURNEY INTO BURMESE SILENCE

MARIE BEUZEVILLE BYLES

What happens when a person practises meditation all day long? The strange day to day adventures both internal and external at various Burmese Buddhist meditation centres are told by the author with more than a dash of humour. She also stayed at nunneries and gained an intimate insight into the heart of Burma's religion and the lives of monks and nuns, while she once happened upon a fantastic fairyland pagoda never before visited by a European.

The author, herself a busy lawyer, is satisfied that perfectly ordinary people who undertake training in Vipassana meditation will find inner peace and happiness despite the rush of Western civilization and without embracing Buddhism.

Demy 8vo. Illustrated. 25s net

WESTERN ENTERPRISE IN FAR EASTERN ECONOMIC DEVELOPMENT

G. C. ALLEN *and* AUDREY G. DONNITHORNE

Political and cultural encounters between the Far East and the West have received considerable attention, but less has been heard of economic contacts. The purpose of this book is to describe as objectively as possible the activities of Western firms in China and Japan from the middle of the nineteenth century, when those countries were opened to foreign trade, until recent times.

The authors discuss the organization of the Western business undertakings, the types of firms concerned and relations between the Westerners and the native economies. The chief branches of economic activity have been covered, namely, merchanting, banking and finance, manufacturing, mining, shipping and internal transport. A dominant theme is the contrast presented by China and Japan in their response to Western enterprise.

The authors, who have lived and studied in the Far East, have obtained much of their information from firms engaged in the Eastern trade as well as from contemporary sources. Their book not only makes a major contribution to the economic history of the Far East, but is also of general interest for the light it throws on the part played by Western business men in economically backward countries.

Demy 8vo. 30s net

GEORGE ALLEN & UNWIN LTD